The Falling Rate of Profit

New Directions/Rethinking Marxism
Series Editors: Bruce Norton and Jack Amariglio

The *New Directions/Rethinking Marxism* series aims to explore and debate the new theories and struggles which will constitute Marxism's contributions to social change in the years ahead. Marxism remains the specter, the antithetical 'other', haunting capitalism – its product as surely as the accumulation of capital and misery have always been. *New Directions/Rethinking Marxism* books will document the new forms, insights and transformative strategies of that radical otherness.

New Directions/Rethinking Marxism is a project of the Association for Economic and Social Analysis, a US-based organization which also publishes the journal *Rethinking Marxism* and holds periodic international conferences on contemporary Marxist thought.

Bringing it All Back Home: Class, Gender and Power in the Modern Household
Harriet Fraad, Stephen Resnick and Richard Wolff

The Falling Rate of Profit
Recasting the Marxian Debate

Stephen Cullenberg

A New Directions/Rethinking Marxism title

Pluto Press
LONDON • BOULDER, COLORADO

First published 1994
by Pluto Press
345 Archway Road, London N6 5AA
and 5500 Central Avenue, Boulder, Colorado 80301, USA

94 95 96   3 2 1

Copyright © 1994 Stephen Cullenberg

The right of Stephen Cullenberg to be identified as the author of this work has been asserted by him in accordance with the Copyright, Designs and Patents Act 1988

British Library Cataloguing in Publication Data
A catalogue record for this book is available from the British Library

Library of Congress Cataloging in Publication Data
Cullenberg, Stephen.
  The falling rate of profit: recasting the Marxian debate / by Stephen Cullenberg.
    153p. 22cm – (New directions/rethinking Marxism)
    Includes bibliographical references and index.
    ISBN 0-7453-0878-3
    1. Profit. 2. Marxian economics.   I. Title. II. Series.
  HB601.C85   1994
  338.5'16–dc20   94-4432
                                                      CIP

ISBN 0 7453 0878 3 hbk

Designed and produced for Pluto Press by
Chase Production Services, Chipping Norton, OX7 5QR
Typeset from author's disk by
Stanford Desktop Publishing Services, Milton Keynes
Printed in Finland by WSOY

Contents

Preface   vii

1   Introduction   1
A Chronological Review of the Debate over the TRPF   3
Epistemology and Theories of the Social Totality   12
Conclusion   17

2   The Hegelian Totality and the Traditional Debate over the Tendency for the Rate of Profit to Fall   19
Holistic Social Theory   21
The Hegelian Totality   24
Historical Materialism   27
The Capitalist Mode of Production and the TRPF   30
The Traditional Debate over the TRPF – A Review   38
Conclusion   49

3   The Debate over the Okishio Theorem and the Cartesian Totality   51
The Linear Price of Production Model of the Economy   53
The Okishio Theorem   58
Critiques of the Okishio Theorem   59
The Cartesian Totality   67
Methodological Individualism   70
Methodological Individualism and Marxian Theory   76
Conclusion   83

4   A Decentered Marxist Approach to Totality and the Contradictory Movement of the Rate of Profit   85
Althusser and the Concept of a Decentered Totality   86
The Decentered Totality of Resnick and Wolff   90
The Decentered Totality: Enterprise and Economy   92
The Contradictory Effect of Accumulation on the Rate of Profit   96
Conclusion   103

Notes and References   108

Bibliography   132

Index   150

Preface

Marx's theory of the falling rate of profit has long been one of the cornerstones of Marxian economic theory. It is still one of the most hotly debated topics in Marxian economics. For some, Marx's theory imparts the dynamic development of capitalism with a dialectic that will eventually lead to capitalism's downfall. For others it is an imprecise or false theory which, together with the 'metaphysics' of Marxian value theory, should be cast aside for more modern and correct theories. At the core of this debate are different conceptions of technical change or accumulation, different theories of value, alternative conceptions of the economy and even different views on the meaning and significance of the rate of profit which is purported to fall or not. At the same time, not far below the surface of the debate are different views on the political significance of the falling rate of profit, which give this debate a particular urgency and vitality. Roughly, these political positions are of two types: (a) if the rate of profit must necessarily fall, that then provides the basis for a revolutionary transformation to socialism, or, alternatively (b) if it doesn't fall, then political action will necessarily be reformist and capitalism can only be slowly, if ever, transcended. It is little wonder, then, that this longstanding debate continues to this day.

Thus the debate over Marx's theory of the tendency for the rate of profit to fall (TRPF) is not simply a debate over the technicalities of value theory, as a cursory reading of the debate might imply. It also concerns at its very foundation issues concerning the ontological structure of social totalities, different senses of value and profit, opposed theories of causality and profoundly different political visions. Indeed, as I argue throughout this book, the debate over the TRPF which has occurred during the latter part of the twentieth century has taken place within the context of two fundamentally different Marxian paradigms, each of which can be identified by their different understandings of the structure of the social totality. On the one hand, the 'traditional' approach to the debate over the TRPF employs a Hegelian approach to the social totality (discussed in detail in Chapter 2), while the more recent debate over the Okishio theorem employs a Cartesian approach to the social totality (discussed in detail in Chapter 3). The debate over the TRPF, then, is not simply a debate over the movement in the rate of profit, but is also at heart a debate over the very philosophical foundations of social theory. In this way, the debate over the TRPF is part of the larger debate taking place in many fields of social theory over whether micro- or macrofoundations is the correct way to construct a theory of society.

The failure to recognize the presence and consequence of these contending Marxian paradigms at work in the larger debate over the TRPF is, as I argue, critical for understanding why after nearly 100 years this debate still remains such an enormously tangled web. The protagonists of various positions in the debate all too often fail to see or appreciate the now widely accepted position that the meaning and significance of concepts are context-dependent, and therefore the meaning of concepts, words or sentences do not stand alone, independent of their particular usage. In particular the Hegelian and Cartesian approaches to social totality impart irreducibly different meanings and significance to the key concepts of debate such as profit, technical change, enterprise and economy. As a result, the issues of contention in one debate become nonissues or literally nonsensical ones in the other, and failure to reach a resolution on what often seem simply to be technical points of logic or mathematics become the frustrating, and then, too often, polemical result.

Despite the fundamental differences in the Hegelian and Cartesian approaches, they share a commitment to reductionist social theory. For the Hegelian approach, the individual agents (capitalists, workers) are understood to carry out the laws of motion of the capitalist economy, conceived as a structured totality. For the Cartesian approach, the capitalist economy is nothing more than the pattern which emerges from the interaction of independently constituted rational agents. For both approaches, therefore, there is no dialectical interaction between part and whole. One of the purposes of this book is to move the debate over the TRPF beyond what I consider to be the now sterile oscillation between theories based on a microfoundational (Cartesian) or a macrofoundational (Hegelian) approach to social theory. In Chapter 4, I develop a 'decentered' approach to the social totality, where either the part is reduced to the logic of the whole, or the whole is understood simply as an aggregation of preconstituted parts. Given this concept of a decentered totality, Chapter 4 then develops an alternative model of the contradictory movement of the rate of profit, with the hope that this alternative formulation can begin to move the debate over the TRPF in new and more fruitful directions.

As the definition of profit used in Marxian economics may not be familiar to all, a final note on the Marxian definition of profit is in order. The concept of profit employed in economic theory as opposed to that used in practical, everyday business settings has widely divergent meanings and significance. In economic theory there are a number of different meanings of profit. Classical economic theory was concerned with profit as a distributional variable, namely the income which the capitalist class earned. Marx's concern, in contrast, was to show how the origin of profit could be found in the unpaid labor of workers (surplus value), and demonstrate how this particular form of capitalist exploitation had much in common with earlier forms of feudal and slave exploitation. Marginal economic theory more or less banishes the concept of profit from its lexicon, and replaces it with the idea of returns to factors of production based on their marginal productivities. Macroeconomic theories are often constructed on a concept of an aggregate after-tax profit rate which is used in theories of growth, investment and savings decisions.

What is common to all these different approaches to profit is that profit is typically modeled as a homogeneous concept across time and space. That is, little institutional detail is incorporated in the different definitions of profit. Different tax laws, accounting protocols and time horizons do not figure in the definition and calculation of profit. Instead, it is generally assumed that changes in the amount or rate of profit will uniformly impact all firms and decision-makers in the economy. Certainly, as any business person knows, there is no single, uniform definition of profit, but rather an array of measures of returns on investment (ROI), profit rates, and so on. Which particular measure of profit is most useful as an indicator of business strategy will depend on, among other things, the specific set of accounting regulations, tax laws, corporate structures and time horizons. While the approach developed in Chapter 4 differs from everyday business measures in the meaning of profit, it has in common with these measures the idea that there is no single definition of profit uniformly accepted by all capitalist enterprises, but that profit is always a contested concept which differs between firms and across time and space.

I want to express my thanks and indebtedness to many people who have read and commented on this book as it took shape over a number of years. This book had its roots in my PhD dissertation at the University of Massachusetts, Amherst and I am extremely grateful for the comments and encouragement from Stephen Resnick and Richard Wolff in the economics department, and to Robert Ackerman in the philosophy department. As this book developed into its final form, Jack Amariglio, David Ruccio and especially Bruce Norton provided detailed comments which were extremely insightful and helped refine my earlier arguments.

CHAPTER 1

Introduction

> This is in every way the most important law of political economy, and the most essential for understanding the most difficult relations. It is the most important law from the historical standpoint. It is a law which, despite its simplicity, has never before been grasped, and even less consciously articulated.
>
> (Marx, 1973, p. 748)

The law of the tendency for the rate of profit to fall (TRPF) remains one of the most important and highly debated issues in all of economics. At issue for economists of all persuasions is the fundamental question of whether as capitalism grows, this very process of growth will undermine its conditions of existence and thereby engender periodic or secular crises.

Nowhere has this debate been more fiercely contested than among Marxist economists. The theoretical and political importance of this debate for Marxist economists has occasioned an often polemical style of argumentation. For example, John Roemer, an ardent critic of those who believe that capitalism has an inherent TRPF, writes that:

> the dogmatism that has been associated with the theory of the 'rising organic composition of capital' has been one of the heaviest palls on the development of a creative Marxian project to study the laws of motion of modern capitalist society. (1981, p. 88)

Strongly opposed to Roemer's position concerning the TRPF, Pat Clawson writes in an equally contentious fashion of those who accept the validity of the Okishio theorem: 'The Marxism of this school consists of little more than translating neo-classical dogmas into Marxist terminology' (1983, p. 109).

This book has two major objectives. The first is to disentangle, and then reconstruct, the longstanding Marxist debate over the TRPF by examining the way in which its various participants conceptualize the relationship between the social totality and its constituent parts. It will be argued briefly in this introduction, and more extensively in the next two chapters, that there have been two *distinct* Marxist theories of totality and methodology present in the debate over the TRPF. Each theory will be distinguished by whether it reduces the social totality to the summation of a set of pre-existing parts, or whether the parts are understood simply to be an expression of the inner nature of the pregiven totality. The former approach is associated with those currently advocating a microfoundations or 'analytical' approach to Marxist social theory.[1] The latter approach is associated with the broadly defined Hegelian tradition within Marxist theory.[2]

A fundamental concern of this book is to demonstrate how distinct theories impart irreducibly different meanings and significance to the various individual concepts which constitute each theory respectively. This irreducibility occurs even though the individual concepts are often called by the same name. Thus the key concepts in the debate over the TRPF, such as economy, enterprise and technical change, take on very different meanings and acquire a different significance depending on the particular Marxist theory in which they are deployed.

The lack of recognition of this important point is a major reason why the debate over the TRPF among Marxist economists has been, and continues to be, waged so vigorously and, more often than not, polemically. Thus the failure to reach a consensus on the issue of the TRPF cannot be attributed simply to the dogmatism of some recalcitrant theorists who refuse to accept more 'modern' approaches to social theory.

The second major objective of this book is to construct an alternative, nonessentialist and nonreductionist theory of the social totality. This alternative will neither reduce the totality to the summation of a collection of independently constituted parts nor suppose the parts to be an expression of a pregiven totality. Instead, a concept of totality will be constructed where neither parts nor totality exist independently from the other. Part and totality exist only as the result of the mutual interaction of each with the other. Therefore there can be no possibility of one acting as the inner essence or fundamental building block of the other.

This alternative construction of the social totality will then be used to begin to reconceptualize the relationship between technical change and the rate of profit. Before outlining in more detail the major arguments of this book, a brief review of some of the most influential Marxist and non-Marxist positions in the debate over the TRPF will be presented. This review is important, in part to give a historical context to the subsequent arguments, and also to highlight the political importance of the various positions taken in the debate.

A brief caveat first is in order. Not surprisingly, one issue of central concern for almost all participants in the debate has been whether or not the rate of profit will fall with capital accumulation. Indeed, some commentators on this debate group people according to whether they feel that the rate of profit tends to fall or not. This is not the approach that is taken in this book. Instead, particular authors will be grouped according to the distinct approaches to the social totality which they adopt. This approach will show how different Marxist theories affect the meanings and significance of the various concepts and issues in the debate. Thus, no defense or claim is being made here that the rate of profit must indeed necessarily fall over time. Nor is any claim being made that the rate of profit cannot fall as a result of accumulation or technical change.[3] As Chapter 4 will stress, the rate of profit will be understood alternatively as overdetermined by all of its conditions of existence. Hence the rate of profit will move in contradictory and nonteleological ways in response to the ceaseless dialectical interaction of it with its conditions of existence, including, among many others, accumulation and technical change.

A Chronological Review of the Debate over the TRPF

Classical political economy was greatly concerned that as capitalism developed there would be a TRPF. It was feared that a stationary state of no growth would result if profits were to fall to a sufficiently low level.[4] In fact, the potential fall in profits was of such central importance to Classical economists that Marx could write 'that it forms the mystery around whose solution the whole of political economy since Adam Smith revolves and the difference between the various schools since Adam Smith consists in different attempts made to solve it' (1981, p. 318). Indeed, the two most influential Classical political economists, Adam Smith and David Ricardo, grounded their respective theories of falling profits on vastly different reasons.[5]

For Smith, it was the sphere of circulation where the reason for a fall in profits was to be found. Smith believed that the increasing wealth of society would engender contradictions which would eventually result in lower profits. Increased wealth in society would bring about an increased competition for this wealth and eventually lower commodity prices as markets became saturated with competitors. In turn, the lower commodity prices would lead to lower profits.

> The increase of stock, which raises wages, tends to lower profit. When the stocks of many rich merchants are turned into the same trade, their mutual competition naturally tends to lower its profit; and when there is a like increase in stock in all the different trades carried on in the same society, the same competition must produce the same effect in them all. (1965, p. 95)

As society grew, the stock of capital employed would expand as far as the extent of the market would allow. Therefore, profit would be at its lowest level in the most advanced or developed society.

> In a country fully stocked in proportion to all the business it had to transact, as great a quantity of stock would be employed in every particular branch as the nature and extent of trade would admit. The competition,

therefore, would everywhere be great, and consequently the ordinary profit as low as possible. (ibid., p. 95)

Thus Smith saw a fall in profit as endemic to the growth, or accumulation, of the capital stock. Furthermore, he understood this fall in profit to be an expression of circulation conditions, that is, the result of capitalist competition.

In contrast to Smith, David Ricardo linked his theory of declining profits to the sphere of production and the decline in the productivity of agricultural labor which he foresaw. Ricardo was extremely critical of Smith's falling rate of profit theory based, as it was, on a supply and demand analysis of competition. According to Ricardo, Smith's theory could explain why the rate of profit tended to an average across markets, but it could not explain why the average would fall. Consequently, instead of basing his theory on the limit of the market, Ricardo sought to show that society's development would lead to a fall in profit as the result of two factors: the decreasing productivity of agricultural labor and the Malthusian population principle.

For Ricardo, profits were a residual from total output left after rent payments were made to landowners and subsistence wages were paid to workers. The amount of the rent payments was determined by the productivity of the marginal land under cultivation. As increasingly marginal land came under cultivation, rent payments would rise on the premarginal land, i.e. that land which had been previously under cultivation. According to the Malthusian population principle, more and more land will be required to come under cultivation as population growth outstrips the available food production. Consequently the productivity of agricultural labor will continually decline, causing rents to landlords to rise and the value of workers' subsistence wages to increase. As a result, the residual profits, will be squeezed. Ricardo concluded that 'The natural tendency of profits is then to fall; for in the progress of society and wealth, the additional quantity of food required is obtained by more and more labor' (1976, p. 71).

Marx was both an admirer and a critic of Ricardo. He was greatly impressed at Ricardo's understanding of the contradictory nature of capitalist growth and its effect on the rate of profit, but he was highly critical of Ricardo's explanation. By grounding his theory of a falling rate of profit in the declining productivity of agricultural labor, Marx claimed that Ricardo 'flees from economics to seek refuge in organic chemistry' (1973, p. 754). In direct opposition to Ricardo, Marx claimed that the rate of profit would fall not because labor becomes less productive but rather because it becomes more productive.

The key to Marx's claim that there was a TRPF as labor became more productive was the crucial distinction he made between constant and variable capital, a distinction which Ricardo did not make. Marx defined the rate of profit to be equal to $S/(C + V)$: where S is surplus value, C is constant capital, and V is variable capital. The rate of profit can be rewritten as $e/(k + 1)$, where e is the rate of exploitation, S/V, and k is the organic composition of capital, C/V. For Marx, capital accumulation implied an increase in the productivity of labor as accumulation took the form of mechanization where machines replaced labor in the production process. In other words, accumulation implied that there was a *tendency* for the organic composition of capital to rise, and therefore there was also a *tendency* for the rate of profit to fall.[6]

Marx pointed out that the fall in the rate of profit was only a tendency which would be mitigated by all manner of countervailing factors. As will be discussed below, the relative importance of tendency versus countertendency has been one of the most important and persistent issues of debate over the years for Marxist economists.[7]

However, before turning to the Marxist debate over the TRPF, it should be pointed out that concern with the possibility of a declining rate of profit has not been limited to Classical or Marxist economists. Although rarely stated explicitly, neoclassical economics contains a theory of a declining rate of profit in its marginal productivity theory of income distribution.[8] According to this theory, in equilibrium, all factors of production will receive a remuneration equal to the value of their marginal products. In particular, the value of the marginal product of capital will be equal to the profit rate. If it is further assumed, as it commonly is, that there are diminishing returns to capital, and that the capital–labor ratio rises over time, then the marginal product of capital must eventually fall and with it will fall the value of the marginal product of capital. As the value of the marginal product of capital falls, the profit rate will fall as the economy adjusts to a new equilibrium.

The long-term, secular trend in the profit rate has also been the object of substantial empirical study by neoclassical economists. William Nordhaus, for one, investigated in the *Brookings Papers* (1974) whether there was a secular decline in the profit share of national income in the post-Second World War US. He concluded that the profit rate had fallen and attributed this fall to a rise in the capital intensity of production as investors shifted funds into industry responding to lower perceived risks of such investments.

As should now be evident, the issue of a falling rate of profit has been a major concern to many different schools of economics. Nowhere, however, has the issue of a TRPF been more intensely examined and debated than by Marxist economists. Indeed, with the possible exception of the debate over Marx's 'transformation problem', the debate over the TRPF has filled more pages in Marxist literature than any other. This debate has also been, and remains, one of the most polemical in Marxian economics.

In order to see what the major issues have been, I will briefly present in roughly chronological order some of the major subdebates in this literature. A more detailed and critical examination of these debates will be presented in Chapters 2 and 3.

One of the first critiques of Marx's theory of the TRPF appeared in a remarkable article by Ladislaus von Bortkiewicz in 1907. 'Value and Price in the Marxian System' (1952), was primarily devoted to a critique of Marx's theory of value in general, and his 'transformation problem' in particular. Almost as an aside, Bortkiewicz also criticized Marx's theory of the TRPF. Most remarkably, he did so in a manner that anticipated by over 50 years both the result and the mode of argument of the Okishio theorem. As will be shown in detail in Chapter 3, this theorem represents one of the most significant recent attempts to criticize and undermine the traditional Marxian claim of a tendency for the rate of profit to decline as capitalism develops.

Bortkiewicz's main argument was that Marx confused value calculations with price calculations when Marx considered the criteria governing technical change. Marx, Bortkiewicz claimed, believed that capitalists adopted a new technique of production so as to raise the average product of labor which would thereby lower the unit values of the wage and capital goods. According to Bortkiewicz, however, a capitalist will only introduce a new technique of production if it raises its profit rate, or equivalently lowers its cost of production, both of which are denominated in terms of prices. Using a linear price of production model, Bortkiewicz demonstrated that once a technical change occurred and a new general rate of profit was established, this new rate of profit could not be lower than the pretechnical change rate of profit. Thus, technical change could not logically lead to a TRPF, and Marx's insight was incorrect.

Bortkiewicz anticipated the Okishio theorem in two important ways. First, he used a linear price of production model of the economy, as used by Okishio himself, and as is commonly used in Sraffian or neoRicardian value theories. Second, he based the criterion for technical change completely on the individual choice of the capitalist. Surprisingly, it would not be until the 1970s that these two types of theoretical strategies would again be commonly deployed together in order to criticize Marx's theory of the TRPF.

Writing at approximately the same time as Bortkiewicz, M. Tugan-Baranovsky also rejected Marx's argument for a TRPF.[9] In particular, Tugan-Baranovsky rejected the TRPF as an acceptable basis for a theory of crisis. Tugan-Baranovsky was, along with Lenin and Struve, a member of the Legal Marxist school in Russia which was prominent around the turn of the century. The Legal Marxists thought that the correct theory of crisis was one based on the anarchy of capitalist competition. They believed that due to the lack of coordination between capitalists, disproportionalities in sales would periodically develop. They rejected the underconsumption theories of crisis of the Legal Populists, which held that capitalism produced too much surplus value, as well as those who held to a theory of crisis based on the TRPF. Instead, they felt that capitalism would tend to produce too little surplus value.

Tugan-Baranovsky's rejection of the TRPF as the basis of a theory of crisis foreshadowed more recent debates in Marxist crisis theory over the political issues and strategies of reform versus revolution. Implicitly, disproportionality theory implied that while capitalism was crisis prone it could be successfully managed and reproduced through state intervention and planning. For disproportionality theory, there was no inherent tendency for surplus value to disappear and hence no necessity for capitalism to collapse. This position was anathema for many, and for Henryck Grossman in particular, as it denied the historical imperative of socialism and therefore, as Grossman felt, the theoretical foundation for a revolutionary politics.

Writing in the late 1920s, Grossman's main object of attack was Rosa Luxemburg's theory of imperialism.[10] Luxemburg believed that capitalism was characterized by a tendency to underconsume, and, therefore, to overproduce surplus value. The tendency for capitalism to overproduce surplus value would in turn create the problem of its realization. Luxemburg thought that capitalists would seek to open up new markets abroad in an effort to realize surplus value. Grossman objected that Luxemburg's analysis misunderstood the primary contradiction of capitalism. Referring to Luxemburg, Grossman wondered incredulously how she could claim that 'Capitalism, whose very goal is the hunt after surplus value, suffers then from "too much" surplus value!' (quoted in Jacoby, 1975, p. 31). Instead, Grossman maintained that crises were brought on by capitalism's tendency to overaccumulate and the concomitant tendency for the rate of profit to fall.

While Grossman was not the first Marxist to write about Marx's TRPF, he was the first neither simply to mention it in passing nor to reject it. After Grossman, the theory of the TRPF became for Marxists as legitimate a theory of crisis as either underconsumption or disproportionality theory.

Paul Sweezy in *The Theory of Capitalist Development*, and Joan Robinson in *An Essay on Marxian Economics*, both originally published in 1942, rejected the validity of Marx's law of the TRPF. Their critique, however, was not one which criticized the TRPF as a basis for crisis, as was Tugan-Baranovsky's. Rather, Sweezy and Robinson each felt that Marx's theory was *logically* incorrect. The reasons for their reaction would frame the major issues of debate in the Marxian literature over the next 25 years.

This debate will be examined in detail in Chapter 2 but a short review will be useful here. Briefly, their argument was twofold. First, both agreed with Marx that accumulation would undoubtedly be characterized by increased mechanization, i.e., in Marx's terms the technical composition of capital would rise. However, they saw no reason why the organic composition of capital, a value (labor–time) magnitude, would necessarily also rise. The reason for their doubt was that mechanization would increase the average product of labor and thereby cause the unit value of the commodity output (the reciprocal of the average product of labor) to fall. If the average product of labor rose in the capital goods industry, then the subsequent fall in the unit value of the capital good could conceivably overwhelm any increase in the mass of the capital goods. Consequently, constant capital could fall rather than rise. There was no *a priori* reason, they insisted, why the counteracting factor of the cheapening of constant capital in value terms could not overwhelm any rise in the technical composition of capital. Therefore, there was no reason why the organic composition of capital could not fall with accumulation and, consequently, the rate of profit rise rather than fall.

Second, assuming a rise in the average product of labor also occurred in the industry producing wage goods, the unit value of the wage goods would also fall. Assuming further a constant real wage, as did Marx, there would be a fall in variable capital. The fall in the variable capital in turn creates the production of relative surplus value and as a result the rate of exploitation would rise. The rise in the rate of exploitation could be theoretically sufficient to offset any putative increase in the organic composition of capital. As both these counteracting tendencies could potentially swamp a rising technical composition of capital, there was no necessary tendency for the rate of profit to fall according to Sweezy and Robinson.

There were many responses to Sweezy's and Robinson's objections to Marx's TRPF but perhaps the two most influential were made by Roman Rosdolsky and Ronald Meek. Rosdolsky in an article in *Kyklos* in 1956 and Meek in *Science and Society* in 1960 each responded in a similar fashion to Sweezy and Robinson. They objected to the possible fall in the organic composition of capital on empirical grounds, and to the possible rise in the rate of exploitation on logical grounds.

Against the potential devaluation of constant capital and the related fall in the organic composition of capital, Rosdolsky argued that the empirical evidence overwhelmingly demonstrated that the mass of capital goods had increased to such an extent that any devaluation of the capital goods could not possibly counteract the rise in the technical composition of capital. Similarly, Meek recognized the theoretical possibility of a falling organic composition of capital. However, he showed through a series of numerical examples in which he examined the effects of an increase in the average product of labor on the organic composition of capital, the rate of exploitation, and the value rate of profit, that only in a very few, and for him unlikely, circumstances would an increase in the average product of labor lower the organic composition of capital so much as to raise the rate of profit.

Sweezy's and Robinson's objection that the rate of exploitation might rise sufficiently to offset the rise in the organic composition of capital was based on a logical error, according to Rosdolsky and Meek. They claimed that due to the absolute limit of the length of the working day (24 hours) the production of surplus value has an impassable limit. Thus, while the organic composition of capital could theoretically rise indefinitely, the increase in the amount of surplus value produced would eventually come up against certain impassable limits. Therefore, the value rate of profit must eventually fall.[11]

In 1958 Joseph Gillman published his book *The Falling Rate of Profit*, whose primary purpose was to test empirically Marx's law of the TRPF using data from the United States. Gillman found that until 1917, roughly what he understood to be the era of competitive capitalism, the rate of profit did indeed fall as the organic composition of capital rose. After 1917, however, he found that the organic composition of capital remained relatively constant while simultaneously the rate of exploitation rose. As a result, the rate of profit actually rose during this period. Gillman insisted that this result was due to the advent of monopoly capital and the increasing difficulty of the realization of surplus value in the post-1917 period. These phenomena brought about a tremendous increase in unproductive expenditures such as advertising, state expenditures, etc. Gillman argued that the law of the TRPF needed to be reformulated in order to account for the changed empirical reality of the increased unproductive expenditures. Consequently he suggested that the formula $(S - U)/(C + V)$, where U is defined to be unproductive expenditures, is the proper measure of the rate of profit. He then recalculated this newly defined rate of profit over the period 1917–39 and found that the rate of profit had indeed fallen over this period, thus verifying, for him, Marx's prediction of a falling rate of profit.

The force of Gillman's empirical work and his claim that monopoly and unproductive expenditures caused the rate of profit to fall, almost immediately spawned a vigorous debate in the journal *Science and Society* over the relationship between capital accumulation and the TRPF in an economy dominated by monopoly capital.[12] It is interesting to note that Gillman emphasized the importance of monopoly and realization problems for capitalism over eight years before Baran and Sweezy's highly influential *Monopoly Capital* (1975). Gillman and Baran and Sweezy arrived at opposite conclusions (for Gillman there was a TRPF, for Baran and Sweezy there was a tendency for the surplus to rise and no tendency for a TRPF), yet there was no mention of Gillman's work in *Monopoly Capital*.

Nobuo Okishio published his highly influential article 'Technical Change and the Rate of Profit' in the *Kobe University Economic Review* in 1961. There would be, however, a 15-year hiatus before what is now known as the Okishio theorem occupied center stage in Marx's debate over the TRPF. Following Bortkiewicz, Okishio criticized Marx's theory of the TRPF on two counts. First, according to Okishio, Marx did not use the correct definition of the rate of profit. Marx defined the rate of profit as $S/(C + V)$ (aggregate surplus value divided by aggregate constant and aggregate variable capital), while he should have used the general rate of profit consistent with what are now known as Sraffian or neoRicardian linear price of production models.

Second, Okishio claimed that Marx misunderstood the nature of capitalist competition. According to Okishio, Marx had argued that capitalists would introduce a new technique of production if it raised the average productivity of labor. Okishio insisted, however, that capitalists are not concerned with productivity *per se*, but instead are concerned with lowering their unit cost of production. Okishio showed in a circulating capital model, assuming a fixed real wage, that a viable technical change (i.e. one that is cost-reducing for the innovating capitalist) would never lead to a fall in the general rate of profit.

For some, this result is the *coup de grace* on any claim that capitalism has an inherent tendency for the rate of profit to fall. For instance, Philippe van Parijs wrote in an important review of the debate over the TRPF that the Okishio theorem 'is so devastating that it deprives all arguments (pro and contra) ... of their relevance' (1980, p. 9). For others, however, the Okishio theorem is part of the debilitating attraction that neoclassical economics has had on an ever increasing number of Marxist economists. Anwar Shaikh and John Weeks have been two of the most persuasive and vehement critics of the Okishio theorem.[13] Both argue that the proponents of the Okishio theorem have adopted the neoclassical assumption of perfect competition. They insist that if this 'nonMarxian' assumption were to be dropped the Okishio theorem would not be valid. The focus of their critique, as well as that of others,[14] has been against either the viability assumption regulating the choice of technique, or the assumption of profit maximization, or both. These critiques propose alternative viability conditions which are claimed to be more consistent with the nature of capitalist competition.

This is broadly where the Marxian debate over the TRPF stands today. The vast majority of the articles published take a position in, or around, the debate over the Okishio theorem. It is fair to say that it has become the central issue of concern, displacing the more traditional issues of debate which occupied Sweezy, Robinson, Meek, Rosdolsky and others for so many years. One reason for this displacement will be suggested in Chapters 2 and 3. It will be argued there that there are two different Marxist theories at work in the 'traditional' debate over the TRPF and in the Okishio debate respectively. These two different theories will be identified by their respective approaches to conceiving the nature of the social totality which I suggest labeling the Hegelian and Cartesian totalities. The argument will be that the traditional debate over the TRPF has taken place on the terrain of the Hegelian totality, while the Okishio debate has been, and is, occurring on the terrain of the Cartesian totality. Thus the prominence which the Okishio debate enjoys today can in large part be attributed to the rejection of the Hegelian totality by Marxist economists in favor of the Cartesian totality.

That the debate over the TRPF has failed to reach a resolution or even to decrease in intensity over the 90 years since Engels first published volume III of *Capital* in 1894 is testament, in part, to the important theoretical issues with which this debate has been concerned. As was briefly outlined above, this debate has at various times been concerned with such key theoretical issues as the crisis tendencies of capitalism, the logical validity of value theory, the effect of monopoly and unproductive expenditures on the accumulation process, and the nature of technical change and capitalist competition. The many twists and turns of the various theoretical positions advanced in the debate attest powerfully, if nothing else, to the openendedness and contradictory nature of all theoretical endeavor.

However important these theoretical issues have been and continue to be, no explanation of this longstanding debate would be complete that did not also recognize its profound political importance for many of the participants in the debate.[15] Very simply, the political issue which is at stake for some is whether capitalism is capable of reform, or whether a revolutionary transformation is needed to alleviate its perceived oppressions.

John Weeks has forcefully made this point. For him, 'What is at stake is whether capitalism is by its very nature stable and capable of sustained dynamism, or whether the accumulation of capital is self-limiting' (1982, p. 62). Whether capitalism is self-limiting or not is an issue of utmost *political* importance for Weeks. He writes that 'the debate over the tendency for the rate of profit to fall does correspond to the debate over revolutionary strategy ... involved here is the debate over the possibility of a peaceful road to socialist transformation' (ibid., p. 62). David Yaffe echoes this sentiment when he states that 'If the capitalist mode of production can ensure, with or without government intervention, continual expansion and full employment, the most important objective argument in support of revolutionary socialist theory breaks down' (1973, p. 187).

How is this link between theory and political practice made? For some theorists, such as Grossman, Weeks, Shaikh and Yaffe,[16] to deny that capitalism has an inherent tendency for the rate of profit to fall is to deny that there are objective revolutionary situations. If a falling rate of profit, and hence crises, are not permanent, built-in features of capitalism's laws of motion, then there is no objective necessity for the transition to socialism.

Crises are then understood to be caused by disproportionalities, underconsumption and/or increasing wages. All such crises can be corrected by an enlightened state adopting the appropriate mix of fiscal and monetary policies. As a result, Marxist proponents of disproportionality, underconsumption or profit-squeeze theories of crisis are very often labeled as left-Keynesians or revisionists by their opponents.

In reaction to this position, it is sometimes argued that to accept that capitalism has immanent tendencies for a falling rate of profit, and therefore breakdown, is to adopt a mechanistic and economistic political perspective. It is argued that such a position denies the effectiveness of conscious political organization. It is obviously highly problematic to make any necessary connection between a particular theory and a consequent political strategy. Nevertheless, these connections are often made in the debate over the TRPF, and made concerning the most important political questions for the theorists involved in the debate. These political questions will be taken up again in Chapter 4.

Epistemology and Theories of Social Totality

There is yet another reason, besides these important theoretical and political ones, why the debate over the TRPF has failed to reach resolution and remains the subject of so much polemical writing. As was briefly alluded to above, there are two *distinct* Marxian theories present in this debate. As a result, the key theoretical terms of profit, enterprise, economy and technical change take on irreducibly different *meanings* and *significance* depending on which Marxian theory deploys them. Not only do these important concepts obtain different meanings and significance as they are deployed in and through the different theoretical approaches, but the major issues of debate in one approach become nonissues, or literally 'nonsensical' ones, in the other. This important point about the presence and incommensurability of fundamentally different theoretical frameworks in the Marxian debate over the TRPF has never before been explicitly articulated. As a consequence, the failure to see the irreducibility of these different theories is, in part, a cause for the debate's continued irresolution and polemical nature.

The claim that different theoretical constructs impart an irreducibly different meaning and significance to the concepts which constitute them derives from a general approach to the philosophy of science and epistemology that has become increasingly influential in recent years. This approach is, in different ways, associated with the work of, among others, Thomas Kuhn, Richard Rorty, Michel Foucault, Jacques Derrida, Donald McCloskey, Stephen Toulmin and Nelson Goodman in the nonMarxist tradition,[17] and Louis Althusser, Barry Hindess and Paul Hirst, Ernesto Laclau and Chantal Mouffe, and Stephen Resnick and Richard Wolff in the Marxist tradition.[18]

There are of course many differences among and between these various theorists, but a common thread running through all their work, a thread which is important for the approach being advocated here, is that they all reject the traditional empiricist and rationalist correspondence theories of epistemology. Rationalist and empiricist epistemologies are based on the belief that theoretical discourse and material reality exist as separate and distinct ontological realms. According to these correspondence epistemologies there exists an *ontological gap* between the theoretical realm and the material realm.

Theoretical discourse is, then, to be spoken or written *about* a separate and disjoint material reality, according to these epistemologies. Theory can only reflect or disclose the independently constituted reality; it does not participate in its constitution. Epistemology's job is to validate the 'truth' content of each theory by examining the correspondence of its theoretical statements with the preexisting material reality. It follows from this perspective that some theories are 'better' or 'more correct' than others insofar as they correspond more closely to the separate and distinct material reality. As theories 'improve' they mirror nature or the social world ever more closely, to borrow a phrase from Rorty.

In contrast, the epistemological position that I will adopt in this book is premised on the idea that there is no ontological gap between theory and material reality. Theoretical discourse is not *about* a separately and distinctly constituted material reality. Instead, theory and material reality are assumed mutually to constitute one another. In the language of Althusser, and Resnick and Wolff,[19] theory and material reality overdetermine one another; neither exists separately and distinctly from the other. According to this view, there is no unique correspondence between theory and reality. Theoretical discourse changes material reality as material reality changes theoretical discourse. If they codetermine (or overdetermine) one another, then it follows that neither one can serve as the standard of truth for the other. A standard of truth requires an independent or absolute point of reference. But in this case the independence has been corrupted by the mutual interaction between theoretical discourse and material reality. Therefore, there is no unique or correct way in which a theory can either be verified or falsified.

Each theory literally *constructs* its own truth, and criteria for the validity of that truth. As theories become more developed and complicated, the theory itself changes and along with it the material reality. This implies that as a theory is *elaborated* the meaning and significance of the previous concepts in the theory change. As all theories are conditioned in part by the material reality, and in part by other theories, this implies that theoretical discourse will be constantly changing, and changing in a contradictory manner, as it responds to the myriad pushes and pulls of the material and theoretical aspects of the world.

This process of the elaboration of concepts has occurred, and continues to occur, in the debate over the TRPF. There are in the debate two distinct Marxist theoretical approaches through which the concept of a social totality is constructed. As a result, each approach has produced different and incommensurable understandings of the relationship between technical change, or accumulation, and the rate of profit. Some issues of debate in one approach are nonissues or literally nonsensical ones in the other approach. For instance, the relationship between the value categories such as the organic composition of capital and the rate of exploitation, of central concern in the traditional debate over the TRPF, is a nonissue in the Okishio debate. In contrast, those participating in the Okishio debate typically operate with a Sraffian value system which does not employ the traditional Marxist value categories, and therefore such concerns over value theory make no sense in the Okishio debate. Similarly, the issue of how a capitalist's choice of technique is to be understood, a major area of contention in the Okishio debate, is of no concern in the traditional debate over the TRPF, because there accumulation is understood to be the inner law of motion governing capitalism, regardless of what individual capitalists 'choose'.

What, then, are the two distinct theoretical approaches present in the debate over the TRPF? As mentioned above, each theory will be identified by the particular way in which it conceptualizes the relationship between a totality and its parts. On the one hand, the *Hegelian totality* will be identified in this book as that approach to understanding the social totality which reduces its parts to an expression of the inner nature, or essence, of the totality. The notion of the Hegelian totality whose parts express the inner essence of society was elaborated and critiqued by Louis Althusser in his attempt to distinguish the Hegelian approach to totality from the Marxist approach.[20]

The *Cartesian totality*, on the other hand, will be identified as that approach to totality which reduces the totality to the summation of its parts. In this case, the social totality can be interpreted metaphorically to resemble a machine whose parts can be examined and understood independently from all the other parts, and from the totality itself.[21]

Each approach to totality, the Hegelian and the Cartesian, makes its presence felt in the debate over the TRPF. The Hegelian totality is the theoretical terrain on which the *traditional* debate over the TRPF has been contested. The Cartesian totality sets the theoretical terrain on which the debate over the *Okishio theorem* has occurred. Insofar as the traditional and Okishio debates have been contested on the basis of their distinct approaches to Marxian theory, there is a fundamental incompatibility between them.

Neither approach is the *obviously correct* one for understanding the relationship between a totality and its parts, nor for understanding the relationship between technical change (accumulation) and the rate of profit. However, each approach produces its distinct relative truth, or understanding, about the social totality in general, and technical change and the rate of profit in particular. As a result, the major issues of contention in one debate, influenced as they are by one particular theoretical approach to totality, may appear incomprehensible or as nonissues in the other approach. This, I argue, is precisely what has happened in the debate over the TRPF. The failure by the participants concerned to recognize the presence of these two distinct theories, and their fundamental incompatibility, has contributed to all manner of theoretical frustrations as well as the periodic polemical outbursts that have so characterized this debate.

The existence of this incompatibility is a result of the process of successive theoretical elaborations of the general conceptualization of the relationship between a totality and its parts. As mentioned above, theories are contradictory and therefore constantly changing as they respond to the changing material reality as well as to changes in other theoretical discourses. As theories change by incorporating new conditions of existence in their discursive space, they distance themselves further and further from other theories with which they once shared a certain degree of commensurability.

This process of elaboration of new conditions of existence and the subsequent distinguishing of theories from one another can be seen in the manner in which the Hegelian and Cartesian totalities reduce whole to part, or *vice versa*. The Hegelian and Cartesian totalities both share a concern with the relationship between whole and parts but they differ over which is to receive causal priority. The new conditions of existence, i.e. the direction of causal reduction (part to whole, or whole to part), already creates irreducible differences between these two theories. In particular, the form of reduction in the Hegelian totality gives rise to an expressive causality, while the opposite form of reduction in the Cartesian approach gives rise to a mechanistic, linear causality. Thus the way in which each theory understands the laws of motion and the dynamic behavior of the parts of any particular theoretical object will be irreducibly different. The Hegelian approach will understand the theoretical object to be the result of the laws of motion of the totality governed by its inner essence. The purpose of its theoretical discourse then is to discover this inner essence and explain how various laws of motion are logically derived from it. The Cartesian approach will understand the theoretical object to be the result of the interaction of the self-constituted parts of the totality. The purpose then of its theoretical discourse will be to understand the logic (rationality) of the parts and then trace out the patterns that emerge (the totality) from their interaction.

A further elaboration of these theories is made in the debate over the TRPF by identifying the part with the capitalist enterprise and the totality with the economy. The object of discourse, i.e. the effect of technical change or accumulation on the rate of profit, is then analyzed respectively in and through the Hegelian totality (the traditional debate over the TRPF) and the Cartesian totality (the Okishio debate). The result is that different and irreducible discursive spaces are constructed through which the two debates take place. For instance, in the traditional debate the economy is typically understood as the capitalist mode of production and the enterprise is usually referred to as 'capital' whose role it is to act out the inner law of the capitalist mode of production, accumulation. For the Okishio debate, however, the economy is the equilibrium configuration which emerges as each enterprise acts as a rational individual capitalist maximizing its profit. The result of this further elaboration is that the issues of debate become radically and irreducibly different between each discursive space. For example, the traditional debate is concerned primarily with discovering the logical contradictions contained in the accumulation process. The debate over the Okishio theorem, however, is in large part concerned with the effect of different assumptions about capitalist rationality on the relationship between technical change and the rate of profit.

There can be no doubt that each debate is cogent and fruitful in its distinct discursive space, but once the participants in the debate unselfconsciously cross over from one space to the other their theoretical analysis and proclamations become nonsensical, or nonissues, or both. For example, after extensively reviewing the traditional debate over the TRPF, Philippe van Parijs introduces and summarily claims that the Okishio theorem has written the obituary for the traditional debate. Van Parijs, however, makes no recognition of the changed theoretical terrain on which his claims are based. Suddenly, his analysis is in terms of rational capitalist choice without any explicit reference to the differences between that approach and the approach that informed the first half of his essay. He ends his essay by exhorting Marxists to abandon their previous beliefs about the TRPF which they held for 'extrascientific' reasons and to 'give way to "scientific" considerations – and stomach the truth' (1980, pp. 12–13). The trouble with this polemical advice is, of course, that as there are a myriad of scientific discourses in the Marxist and nonMarxist tradition, which one does he mean?

One major objective of this book is to demonstrate how these two different Marxist theories present in the debate over the TRPF can be distinguished on the basis of how they conceptualize the social totality. However, another equally important objective is to produce an alternative analysis of the relationship between technical change and the rate of profit. This alternative analysis will be informed by a notion of totality which differs significantly from the Hegelian and Cartesian approaches. The concept of a *decentered totality* will be developed in which neither the part nor the whole are reduced to an effect of the other. Instead, part and whole will be understood mutually to constitute one another. Associated with this concept of a decentered totality is the concept of a multi-dialectical or overdetermined causality. This concept of causality can be understood by recognizing that each part, or process, is constituted by all the other processes of the totality. Therefore, each process exists as the effect of the totality of its constituent processes. There can be no hierarchy of causes as in the Hegelian and Cartesian approaches as each process emerges, comes into existence, as the simultaneous effect of all of its conditions of existence. Furthermore, as each process is uniquely constituted, each exists in complex contradiction as it responds to the different pushes and pulls of its conditions of existence.

In particular, Chapter 4 will develop a class analytic model of the capitalist enterprise where the enterprise will be understood to be a decentered totality. Each enterprise, therefore, will be the site of a unique set of economic, political and cultural conditions of existence. As the enterprise will be understood to be a decentered totality there can be no inner law of motion governing it, or pregiven rationality informing it. Instead, the enterprise participates in and responds to changes in its internal class and nonclass structure, as well as its external economic, political, cultural and class environment. The enterprise and its environment coexist always in a contradictory, nonteleological, multi-dialectical interplay.

In this instance, the value rate of profit will be understood to be overdetermined by the contradictory movement of all of its conditions of existence, not simply by accumulation or technical change. As a result, based on this model it will be possible to expand the debate over the TRPF to include political, cultural, and economic factors not normally considered relevant to the movement of the value rate of profit. On a related point, the rate of profit will not be understood as a reflection, or expression, of the state of the economy's accumulation process as in the traditional debate. Nor will the rate of profit be understood as the focus of capitalist rationality, to be maximized. Instead, the value rate of profit will be understood to be one measure of the class relations of a capitalist enterprise at a particular moment in time. The precise meaning and significance of this measure will depend, as with all statistical indicators, on the conditions of existence which overdetermine its value. No unambiguous or straightforward interpretation, political or otherwise, of the state of class relations can be directly read from movements in the value rate of profit.

Conclusion

This chapter has introduced the major arguments of the book. The longstanding debate over the TRPF is not simply one long, homogeneous debate, but rather has contained two, broadly defined approaches to Marxian theory. These approaches can be identified respectively by their Hegelian and Cartesian approaches to totality. These different theories impart irreducibly different meanings and significance to their major constituent concepts. Therefore, the concepts of economy, enterprise and technical change (accumulation), acquire and play very different roles, depending on whether they are deployed in the traditional or Okishio debates over the TRPF.

A further concern of this chapter has been to introduce briefly the alternative concept of a decentered totality. This will be developed in Chapter 4 in order to reconceptualize the relationship between technical change and the rate of profit.

The remainder of this book will develop in detail the Hegelian, Cartesian, and decentered approaches to social totality as briefly outlined in this introductory chapter. Each concept of totality will be elaborated and the connections drawn between technical change and the rate of profit in the context of each respective approach to totality.

CHAPTER 2

The Hegelian Totality and the Traditional Debate over the Tendency for the Rate of Profit to Fall

The traditional debate over the TRPF has been informed by a distinct type of Marxian theory which can be identified by the way that one understands the relationship between a social totality and its parts. As will be argued in detail in this chapter, the Hegelian totality underlies the debate over the TRPF. The presence of the Hegelian totality imparts to this debate a distinct way of making sense of the relationship between accumulation and the rate of profit, and in turn defines the terms and issues of debate.

The Hegelian totality is a particular instance of the tradition of social explanation which is known as holism, which assumes that the whole is a pregiven, structured totality. That is, the whole is presumed to exist prior to and independent from its parts. The parts express in and through their existence the inner essence of the totality. The totality is Hegelian in the sense that its inner essence is dynamic and contradictory. The contradictory nature of the inner essence means that the essence unfolds in a dialectical manner guided by a telos, or end. This dialectical unfolding of the inner essence of the Hegelian totality is often referred to as the law of motion of the totality.[1]

The Hegelian totality gives rise to a particular type of causality, an expressive causality. Expressive causality means that the parts in the totality act out, or express, their role according to the pregiven nature of the totality. The whole causes the parts. The parts do not cause the whole. In this sense, the Hegelian totality is associated with a particular form of essentialist causality.

The logical or causal structure of the Hegelian totality is conditioned by a rationalist epistemology. The truth of the whole is to be discovered not in the empirical reality of the world, but rather in the logical coherence of theory. According to rationalist epistemology, human reasoning is structured in a manner isomorphic to the ontological structure of the world. The mind is therefore adequate to the task of apprehending the causal, or rational, order of material being. Nature, and society, is consequently knowable through reason. Thus the role of social explanation in the context of the Hegelian totality is to discover and refine the logical connections of the various parts of the totality once its inner essence is defined.[2]

The Hegelian totality has fundamentally shaped the terrain on which the traditional debate over the TRPF has occurred. In this debate, capitalism has been understood to be a totality whose inner essence is contradictory. The role of the capitalist enterprise, conceived to be one of the constituent parts of the totality, is to accumulate. The accumulation process, however, is understood to be a contradictory one, and the TRPF is understood to be one manifestation of this contradiction. It is the surface appearance of capitalism's inner essence, accumulation.

The traditional debate over the TRPF has engaged some of the most influential Marxist economists of the last 50 years. These economists include Henryck Grossman (1992), Maurice Dobb (1945, 1959), Paul Sweezy, (1970, 1974, 1981), Joan Robinson (1959, 1963, 1978), Ernest Mandel (1970a), Ronald Meek (1960), Roman Rosdolsky (1956) and H.D. Dickinson (1957). The debates among and between these economists have been over numerous issues, but one concern has held pride of place over the whole span of debate. The primary focus of dispute has concerned the exact, or 'correct' relationship between Marx's value categories such as the organic composition of capital, the rate of exploitation and the value rate of profit.

The focus of the traditional debate on the logical connections between the Marxian value categories is not surprising once it is realized that the debate is so intimately informed by the Hegelian totality. In particular, the rationalism of the Hegelian totality has critically influenced the issues of concern in the traditional debate over the TRPF. Once capitalism's inner essence, accumulation, is discovered, then the role of the Marxist economist is to logically unfold the connections and contradictions of the accumulation process.

The traditional debate over the TRPF begins from the assumption that the inner essence of capitalism is accumulation. There is no disagreement over, and hence no debate about, whether or not accumulation is the driving force of capitalism. That is accepted by all. Instead the debate concerns the unpacking of the logical implications of the accumulation process.

It is also interesting to note that this longstanding debate has been almost exclusively concerned with theoretical issues. In the 50 years or so of debate there have been only four major studies which have attempted to empirically investigate whether there has indeed been a TRPF. These empirical studies, by Gillman (1958), Mage (1963), Chung (1981) and Moseley (1991), have had little influence in the larger debate over the TRPF.[3] Again, this is not surprising given the rationalism of the traditional debate over the TRPF, shaped as it is by the Hegelian totality. For a rationalist, empirical data cannot refute a properly specified theory. Only a better theory, or more logically coherent one, can displace another theory.[4]

The remainder of this chapter is organized as follows. The next section will briefly review the holistic tradition of social explanation in order to show how the Hegelian totality is a special, and influential, form of holistic thought. After discussing the salient features of the Hegelian totality, the Marxian theory of historical materialism will be reviewed to show how it has incorporated the Hegelian totality.

It is then argued that the traditional debate over the TRPF has been profoundly shaped by the concept of a Hegelian totality. It is argued that the traditional debate assumes that capitalism is a totality whose contradictory inner essence is accumulation. The last section of this chapter draws out some of the more important issues of dispute in the traditional debate. These issues concern the logical connections between the Marxian value categories of the organic composition of capital, the rate of exploitation and the value rate of profit.

Holistic Social Theory

The Hegelian totality is part of the holistic tradition of social theory. As a first approximation, holism can be defined as that mode of social explanation which assumes that the whole exists prior to, and independent from, its parts. The whole is understood to be a structured totality or a unity which is organized by an inner essence. The inner essence imparts on the totality a purpose and/or logical cohesion. The parts of the totality have meaning only as they are considered in and through their place or function in the totality. The parts of the totality are sometimes referred to as the surface manifestation, or appearance, of the inner essence of the totality.[5]

Holistic theories may, but do not necessarily, posit a series of successive totalities where the succession of totalities is governed by an inner law of motion. Neither do all holistic theories necessarily posit some goal, or telos, as the end of history. These dynamic qualities of holistic theories are, however, prominent in Hegel's philosophy of history, as well as in the Marxian theory of historical materialism.

The history of holistic social theory goes at least as far back as the Greeks. Aristotle, for instance, felt that all identifiable things have an inner nature, or *ergon*. Scott Meikle, in his provocative book, *Essentialism in the Thought of Karl Marx* (1985), discusses the meaning of Aristotle's *ergon*. He writes that 'Properly understood, the *ergon* of a thing, creature or system is ... often an indispensable determinant in our efforts to find out what the item really *is*, and to reveal its nature' (1985, p. 169). The *ergon* of something, then, for Aristotle is that which defines it, gives it purpose, which reveals its inner nature.

Aristotle's thought has often been interpreted in a teleological manner. While it is true that Aristotle often referred to a telos in nature and society, his concept of telos was not one to which everything in the cosmos was tending. Rather, as Meikle (1985) and Martin Jay (1984) have pointed out, Aristotle's telos was meant to be the inner nature or essence of a thing. Indeed, Aristotle in volume 2 of the *Physics* (1936, p. 194a 28f) wrote that 'the "form" or *eidos*, *telos* or end or final cause, *ergon* or "function", and *to ti en einai* or essence of a being are the same thing, for "a thing's nature is its end or final cause"'.

Aristotle focused on the state as the most important form of social totality (Jay, 1984, p. 25). He wrote in the *Politics* that:

> The state is by nature clearly prior to the individual, since the whole is prior to the parts. The proof that the state is a creation of nature and prior to the individual is that the individual, when isolated, is not self-sufficing; and therefore he is like a part in relation to the whole. (1920, p. 1253a)

While Aristotle believed that all identifiable things, whether organic or inorganic, individuals or states, were to be considered as wholes with identifiable essences or *ergons*, he did not have a theory of history as the unfolding of a purposeful, teleological process. Jay makes this point in his important book *Marxism and Totality*.

> What Greek thought lacked, however, was a belief that history could be understood as a progressively meaningful whole with a beginning, middle and end. Preferring to see time repeating itself in infinite cycles without any progress ... the Greeks failed to develop what might be called an optimistic, 'longitudinal' concept of totality. (1984, p. 26)

As Jay makes clear, it was not until St Augustine and the development of Christian doctrine that such a concept of progressive, or longitudinal, development was introduced. This teleological aspect of holistic thought was adopted by Hegel in his philosophy of history and eventually adopted by many Marxists in the form of historical materialism. It is interesting to note that historical materialism, according to the account given here, is in part directly descendant from early Christian thought.

Holistic thought has also been influential in the social sciences. Gestalt psychology is one notable form of holism. In sociology, Durkheim (1958) represents a prominent and influential example of holistic social theory. In economics, the German 'historical school' inspired by Gustav Schmoller and Adolph Wagner rejected the marginalism that was developing around the turn of the twentieth century. The economics of Keynes can be understood as an holistic alternative to the microeconomic foundations of much of modern neoclassical economic theory.[6] The German historical school gave rise to a form of social explanation known as historicism.[7] The debate over historicism became quite strident in the hands of Karl Popper (1944a, 1944b, 1945) and Friedrich Hayek (1942, 1943, 1944) in the 1940s. It was this debate which was to trumpet into dominance the methodological individualist approach in economics and other social sciences. Jay writes that 'Historicism saw history in holistic terms, either as a universal process with a coherent meaning or as a series of discrete totalities that were separate nation-states of world history' (1984, p. 74). Hayek similarly saw historicism as a form of developmental holism.

> The naive view which regards the complexes which history studies as given wholes naturally leads to the belief that their observation can reveal 'laws' of development of these wholes. The belief is one of the most characteristic features of scientific history which under the name historicism was trying to find the empirical basis for a theory of history, and to establish necessary successions of definite 'stages' or 'phases', 'systems' or 'styles' which followed each other in historical development. (1943, p. 58)

Hayek's description of historicism could equally be a description of Hegel's theory of history where the idealist spirit guides history through its successive stages, as well as a description of the Marxian theory of historical materialism where the contradiction between the forces and relations of production is the driving force of history.

Popper links historicism to organicism in *The Poverty of Historicism* (1957). He writes there that 'there is a close connection between historicism and the so-called *biological or organic theory* of social structures – the theory which interprets social groups by analogy with living organisms' (1957, p. 19). It was Popper who, in *The Open Society and Its Enemies* (1950), launched one of the most concerted attacks on Marxism as an insidious form of holistic thought. For Popper, Marxism must be rejected because its holism suppressed the importance of the individual. He argued that social science should adopt a methodological individualism in order to guard against this danger.

There have also been numerous holistic theories in the history of the natural sciences. In evolutionary biology, vitalism was an influential theory for a time (Mayr, 1982, p. 52). In physics David Bohm has put forth a holistic theory of the implicate, or unfolding, order in opposition to the atomistic and particle theories of traditional physics (1983).

However, it was Hegel's system, his logic and his philosophy of history, which probably has been the most fully developed and explicit holistic theory. It has certainly been Hegel's work, with its focus on the dialectical unfolding of successive and progressively more developed totalities throughout history, that has had the most influence on the Marxian tradition. Indeed, some versions of historical materialism have not been much more than a straightforward materialist application of Hegel's idealist theory of history.

The Hegelian Totality

There can be no doubt that Hegel had a profound influence, first on Marx and subsequently on the Marxian tradition. Regardless of how Hegel's relationship to and influence on Marx and the Marxian tradition is understood, his presence, in one form or another, is constantly felt.[8] In particular, the traditional debate over the TRPF can be understood as squarely within the context of the Hegelian totality, as developed in this chapter. To miss this insight, and the consequences that follow from it, is to miss something vital about this debate. It is to miss the discursive and epistemological specificity of the debate; it is to miss the critically distinct meanings and significance which the key terms in this debate acquire; and it is to miss the very logic of the debate and the issues which are confronted therein. Given the importance of these points, some of the more relevant features of Hegel's system as it pertains to Marxian theory in general, and the question of the TRPF in particular, will be developed below.

Perhaps the aspect of the Hegelian system which has had the most influential effect on the Marxist tradition can be captured by Hegel's famous aphorism in the preface to the *Phenomenology of the Spirit*: 'The truth is the whole' (1979, p. 11). The idea of the supremacy of the whole over its parts has been a cornerstone of much Marxian theory, and one which owes its original masonry largely to Hegel.

This fact has not gone unrecognized by Marxists. The early Lukács, for example, claimed that what distinguishes Marxism from bourgeois science are not any substantive issues, but rather its method. In his essay, 'The Marxism of Rosa Luxemburg', Lukács made this point forcefully, and he did not hesitate to give credit to Hegel. He wrote there that:

> It is not the primacy of economic motives in historical explanation that constitutes the decisive difference between Marxism and bourgeois thought, but the point of view of the totality ... The category of totality, the all-pervasive supremacy of the whole over the parts is the essence of the method which Marx took over from Hegel and brilliantly transformed into the foundations of a wholly new science. (1971, p. 27)

The power of Lukács' analysis helped to create a Hegelian school of Marxists in Europe and the US which has had a tremendous influence on Marxist theory and politics.[9] Hegelian Marxism has certainly been one of the most influential schools of Marxism in the twentieth century, yet it is not without its critics. Althusser, for one, has criticized the Hegelian Marxists for being teleological and essentialist.[10] There is certainly little doubt that Hegel's system itself was guided by the belief in an inner essence moving teleologically through history. To what extent subsequent Marxist theorists also employ a teleological theory of history is a matter of some dispute, and need not be of concern here.

In order to understand the teleological nature of the Hegelian system, it must be recognized that the dialectic for Hegel is synonymous with the whole. For Hegel, the understanding of truth requires a recognition that all that exists, exists in process. Hegel's ontology is based on the principle of movement; reality is a ceaseless process of change. The dialectic, Hegel argues, is the only way in which this movement can be understood and expressed. Each step, phase, stage, or *moment*, in the dialectical triad of affirmation–negation–supersession is required for movement to occur. For Hegel, the concept of the dialectic, and only the dialectic, captures and expresses this process.

Each Hegelian triad defines a particular totality. Each totality, however, is fleeting in that it contains within it the seeds of its own transformation. For Hegel, this continual process of renewal and disappearance is not simply an anarchic jumble of motion, but rather it has a purpose or goal. That is, the dialectic is a constantly changing totality guided by a purposeful inner principle, or essence, and therefore directed toward an end, or telos. Althusser aptly labeled Hegel's dialectic of development the Hegelian totality, in a manner similar to that being used in this book.

> The *Hegelian Totality* is the alienated development of a simple unity, of a simple principle, itself a moment in the development of the Idea: so, strictly speaking, it is the phenomenon, the self-manifestation of this simple principle which persists in all its manifestations, and therefore even in the alienation which restores its restoration. (1979, p. 203)

Thus, all that exists is nothing more than the phenomenal appearance of the inner essence governing its movement. As all phenomena are moments in one or another of the stages of the dialectic, each moment is an expression of the logic of the essence. This relationship between the whole (the dialectic) and its parts (moments in the dialectic) gives rise to what Althusser, again, has called an expressive form of causality.

> ... it presupposes in principle that the whole in question can be reducible to an *inner essence*, of which the elements of the whole are then no more than the phenomenal form of expression, the inner principle of the essence being present at each point in the whole, such that at each moment it is possible to write the immediately adequate equation: *such and such an*

element (economic, political, legal, literary, religious, etc., in Hegel) = *the inner essence of the whole*. (Althusser and Balibar, 1979, pp. 186–7)

The particularity of each part, as well as its laws of motion, is given to it by the whole and the part's location in that totality. It is not other parts which independently cause any particular part to change, rather it is the preexisting whole and its inner principle which cause, or give expression to, each part. Thus Althusser once more can write that Hegel, 'borrowing from Montesquieu the idea that in a historical totality all concrete determinations, whether economic, political, moral, or even military, express one single principle, ... conceives history in terms of the category expressive totality' (1975, p. 182).

Hegel applied his dialectical system to history in his study *The Philosophy of History* (1956). He argued there that history was a rational process guided by an inner logic or essence. The essence of history is what Hegel called the *world spirit*. History is the record of the development through successive stages of the spirit as the spirit tends inexorably towards its telos, the Absolute Spirit.

The spirit for Hegel was not something mystical or transcendental. For Hegel, each nation in a particular historical epoch has a national character, something that transcends the summation of the personalities of the individuals who make up the society. The national character is the spirit of the nation. Humankind, for Hegel, is guided by one overarching goal which is the attainment of the absolute self-awareness of one's place in nature. In the *Philosophy of History* Hegel argued that history can be divided roughly into three epochs according to different levels of self-awareness.

The Oriental world is characterized by an undifferentiated unity.[11] Here, one lives in blissful ignorance, as it were. Humans do not recognize their separateness from nature and therefore do not struggle over it. In the Greek world, however, life is characterized by a differentiated disunity (ibid., p. 1978). Humankind now recognizes that it is distinct from nature and proceeds to struggle among itself over the control of nature's bounty. One is now aware of one's place in the world, but self-awareness of how to live in harmony with nature and others has not yet been discovered. Finally, in the modern world as exemplified by the Prussian state, Hegel argued that humankind is approaching a state of differentiated unity (ibid., p. 1978). One recognizes one's separateness from nature and has learned to live harmoniously with this awareness.

For Hegel, this process of attaining self-awareness is the central problem of human history. It is what imparts a particular character or spirit to different nations and different epochs. It is the telos of all history. Hegel writes that '*the final cause of the World at large,* we allege to be the *consciousness* of its own freedom on the part of Spirit, and *ipso facto,* the *reality* of that freedom' (1956, p. 19). The consciousness of freedom that Hegel speaks about is nothing more than the full awareness of one's true relationship to a distinct natural world. It is the attainment of this awareness or freedom which is the idea, or goal, of spirit. The progressive envelopment of the truth of the Absolute Spirit has been the driving force of history since earliest times.

> The History of the World begins with its general aim – the realization of the Idea of Spirit – only in an *implicit* form that is, as Nature; a hidden, most profoundly hidden, unconscious instinct; and the whole process of History (as already observed) is directed to rendering this unconscious impulse a conscious one. (ibid., p. 25)

Truth is nothing more than the discovery of this process of unfolding. Truth therefore is never stationary because as soon as one dialectical process ends, a new one begins. As mentioned above, history is the record of the continual succession of one whole (dialectic) after another, one truth after another in the process of humankind's self-awareness which ends only in the attainment of Absolute Truth in and through the Absolute Spirit.

Returning to Hegel's aphorism, 'The truth is the whole', it can now be seen that this truth is revealed in the dialectical development of history. It is the dialectic which is the whole. The dialectic is that which guarantees that history is a continual search for absolute self-awareness, for the Absolute Spirit. Herein lies the teleology of the Hegelian system as well as its dialectical holism.

The Hegelian theory of history has been very influential in the Marxist tradition. In particular, the Marxian theory of historical materialism is heavily indebted to Hegel. In turn, through this indebtedness, the Hegelian totality has shaped the traditional debate over the TRPF. The next section discusses the Marxian theory of historical materialism.

Historical Materialism

Hegel's *Philosophy of History* (1956) had a profound impact on Marx and the Marxist tradition. As is well known, Marx's relationship to Hegel has been the subject of enormous debate.[12] It is not the purpose of this section to describe, or enter into, that debate. Rather, the focus in this section will be on the 'stylized facts' of historical materialism, in order to lay the groundwork for a 'reading' of the traditional debate over the TRPF.

The 'standard' interpretation of historical materialism is usually based on the belief that Marx stood an idealist Hegel on his head. That is, Marx accepted the dialectical structure of Hegel's theory of history, but substituted a materialist essence for Hegel's idealist spirit as the driving force of history. For Marx, it was the development of the contradictions of the economic base, rather than humanity's increasing self-awareness, through which society developed in successive stages. In particular, according to historical materialism it was the contradiction between the forces and the relations of production which gave rise to history's inner law of motion.

The canonical text of historical materialism is Marx's preface to *A Contribution to the Critique of Political Economy* (1970). There, in a page and a half, Marx outlines what has been one of the most theoretically and politically influential ideas in the last century. Marx divides society into two broad structures: the economic structure, or base, and the noneconomic structure, or superstructure. The economic base is composed of the articulation of the forces and relations of production. The forces of production are the raw materials, tools, machinery, technology, etc. which are used in the production of use values. The relations of production reflect the class relations of society; 'the existing relations of production or ... the property relations' (1970, p. 21). The superstructure, commonly understood, is the totality of institutions which comprise the social, political and intellectual life of society.[13]

Marx, as did Hegel, understood society to be a structured totality. However, while it was the development of the world spirit which structured society for Hegel, it was the development of the contradiction between the forces and the relations of production which structured and transformed society for Marx. In reference to Hegel, Marx in a famous passage writes that 'It is not the consciousness of men that determines their existence, but their social existence that determines their consciousness' (ibid., p. 21). That is, a materialist Marx appears to be standing an idealist Hegel on his head. In the famous postface to the second edition of volume I of *Capital*, Marx distances himself from Hegel in what must be one the most controversial brief passages of Marx's methodology. He writes:

> My dialectical method is, in its foundations, not only different from the Hegelian, but exactly the opposite to it. For Hegel, the process of thinking, which he even transforms into an independent subject, under the name of 'the Idea', is the creator of the real world, and the real world is only the external appearance of the idea. With me the reverse is true: the ideal is nothing but the material world reflected in the mind of man, and translated in the forms of thought .... The mystification which the dialectic suffers in Hegel's hands by no means prevents him from being the first to present its general forms of motion in a comprehensive and conscious manner. With him it is standing on its head. It must be inverted, in order to discover the rational kernal within the mystical shell. (1976, pp. 102–3)

The Hegelian Totality

For Marx, it is the contradictions embedded in the economic base driven by the development of the productive forces which give the dialectic its 'general forms of motion', driving both the material development of society and *pari passu* society's consciousness. As the productive forces of society develop, the existing social relations of society turn into so many fetters on their further development. In the *Communist Manifesto* (1982) Marx and Engels describe this development in reference to the transformation of feudalism to capitalism.

> At a certain stage in the development of these means of production and of exchange, the conditions under which feudal society produced and exchanged, the feudal organization of agriculture and manufacturing industry, in a word, the feudal relations of property became no longer compatible with the already developed productive forces; they became so many fetters. They had to be burst asunder; they were burst asunder. (ibid., p. 14)

Each distinct form of society, or mode of production, is then a Hegelian totality as each develops according to its inner essence. As the forces of production develop, this development impels society to a new, higher mode of production. The mode of production is higher in the sense that it retains, in Hegelian fashion, its previous history while developing according to its new laws of motion. Each mode of production transcends, rather than simply replaces, a previous, less developed mode. Marx makes this point in *A Contribution to the Critique of Political Economy* where he writes:

> No social order is ever destroyed before all the productive forces for which it is sufficient have been developed, and new superior relations of production never replace older ones before the material conditions for their existence have matured within the framework of the old society. (1970, p. 21)

History is thus the record of the trajectory of successive, distinct modes of production. For Marx, 'In broad outline, the Asiatic, ancient, feudal, and modern bourgeois modes of production may be designated as epochs marking progress in the economic development of society' (ibid., p. 21). Marx felt that the bourgeois mode of production, capitalism, would be the last antagonistic mode of production. Capitalism would play a progressive role in history insofar as it would lay the basis for the transition to communism. The development of the forces of production in capitalism would eventually and immutably create the conditions for its demise. Marx and Engels conclude part I of the *Communist Manifesto* by declaring that:

> The development of modern industry, therefore cuts from under its feet the very foundation on which the bourgeoisie produces and appropri-

ates products. What the bourgeoisie therefore produces, above all, are its own grave-diggers. Its fall and the victory of the proletariat are equally inevitable. (1982, p. 21)

With the victory of the proletariat and the emergence of a communist mode of production, 'The prehistory of human society accordingly closes with this social formation' (Marx, 1970, p. 22). In other words, communism is the telos of history whose advent brings with it the end of contradiction, i.e. the end of class antagonisms. Communism plays the same role for historical materialism as the Absolute Spirit does for Hegel in his philosophy of history. It is the goal to which society is progressing. A goal where contradiction ceases. A goal where the 'prehistorical' forms of antagonism reach their resolution and disappear.

This interpretation of historical materialism has been very influential within the Marxian tradition. The idea that history in general, and capitalism in particular, was a totality unfolding according to its inner laws of motion towards the telos of communism was very prevalent among the members of the Second International.[14] Historical materialism provided the theoretical backdrop for the spirited debate between Plekhanov, Kautsky, Bernstein and many others over whether capitalism had an inherent tendency towards breakdown. An economistic Marxist orthodoxy developed out of these debates in the Second International, an orthodoxy which would dominate Marxism until the 1970s. In particular, two exemplary instances of the Hegelian influence within Marxism were Joseph Stalin's *Dialectical and Historical Materialism* (1940), which had enormous worldwide influence, and Maurice Cornforth's *Historical Materialism* (1954) which was very important in England as well as in communist parties the world over.

This orthodoxy of economism permeated all areas of Marxism but was perhaps nowhere more prevalent than in Marxist economics. And, within Marxist economics, it was crisis theory especially which was characterized by an economic determinism. Capitalism's inner law of motion, accumulation, was understood to be a contradictory and crisis laden process. The object of Marxist crisis theory was, and still is for some, to lay bare the contradictory tendencies and laws of motion of capitalist accumulation in order to facilitate the transition to communism. And, without doubt the most influential Marxist theory of crisis, certainly the one which has received the most attention in the literature, has been that associated with the theory of the TRPF due to an increasing organic composition of capital.[15]

The Capitalist Mode of Production and the TRPF

The traditional debate over the TRPF can be understood in the context of the Hegelian totality as developed above. The Hegelian totality, it will be remembered, assumes that society is to be understood as a pregiven, structured whole which exists prior to, and independent from its parts. The totality is governed by an inner essence, or law of motion, which manifests itself in and through the various parts of the totality. The totality is Hegelian because this inner essence is understood to be contradictory, meaning that each totality contains within it the potential for, and necessity of, its eventual supersession. Thus, history is to be understood as a progression of successive totalities. Furthermore, history is understood to have a goal, or telos, to which it is progressing.

For the traditional debate over the TRPF, capitalism, or alternatively, the capitalist mode of production, is understood to be a Hegelian totality in the above sense. The capitalist mode of production is conceived to exist prior to and independent from its constituent parts. The relevant part for the debate over the TRPF is the capitalist enterprise, which is variously referred to as the capitalist, capitalist firm, or simply 'capital'. Accumulation is capitalism's inner law of motion and it is capital's role to express this essence. Accumulation is a contradictory process which is manifested in part by the law of the TRPF.[16]

That capitalism is conceived to be a totality means that capitalism is understood to be a specific mode of production with its own inner laws of motion. The exact definition of a mode of production differs from author to author, but all stress that the capitalist mode of production consists of an *articulation* of the forces and relations of production. A typical definition is given by Fine and Harris:

> The capitalist mode of production is defined by forces of production (techniques) and relations of production and an articulation between the two all of which are specific to capital. The articulation between forces and relations is such that the relations of production are determinant. (1979, p. 13)

Similar definitions are given by Althusser (1979) and Hindess and Hirst (1977a).[17] Other definitions stress the causal primacy of the forces of production over the relations of production. Maurice Cornforth, for example, gives primacy to the forces of production in his 'orthodox' approach to Marxian theory (1954). G.A. Cohen also privileges the forces of production in his influential defense of Marxian theory which uses the techniques of analytical philosophy (1978). Indeed, as argued above, Marx can be interpreted as giving primacy to the forces of production over the relations. Despite their differences over whether the forces or the relations of production are causally primary, all the above authors implicitly share the notion of capitalism as a structured, Hegelian totality as this concept is being used here.

Michael Lebowitz describes in detail the notion of capitalism as a Hegelian totality. He writes that:

> Capital [capitalism] must be established as a totality, an organic whole, in which all presuppositions are shown to be results .... Through a process of deduction, the logical interconnection of all parts of the whole must be demonstrated, thereby permitting no elements to appear as external, extrinsic, interdependent, indifferent, exogenous to the system – but, rather as 'distinctions within a unity'. In this manner, the intrinsic tendencies, the immanent laws, of the totality can be ascertained; and, this establishment of the inner, the essence, must precede the investigation and elaboration of the necessary forms of existence, of the totality, the multiplicity of its outward forms, and also the manner in which the inner tendencies are manifested and executed on the surface. (1982, p. 41)

Lebowitz makes clear in this statement that analysis must proceed from the totality to its surface manifestations. It is necessary to first grasp the inner essence of the totality before its multi-faceted appearances on the surface of society can be analysed and theoretically comprehended. Once the inner essence is ascertained, the role of the analyst is then *logically to deduce* the interconnection of all the parts of the whole. As will be shown below, this is exactly the discursive format the traditional debate over the TRPF takes. After accepting that the inner law of motion of capitalism is accumulation, the debate over the TRPF has concerned itself with how this law is manifested on the surface of society in and through the movements of the Marxian value categories such as the organic composition of capital, the rate of exploitation and the value rate of profit.

The inner law of motion of capitalism, accumulation, finds expression in and through the capitalist enterprise which is understood to be capitalism's relevant part. The capitalist enterprise is variously referred to in the literature as 'capital', the capitalist or the capitalist firm. Regardless of the exact terminology used, the capitalist enterprise is understood to be the site, the surface part, where the contradictory law of accumulation acts itself out. The capitalist enterprise accumulates because that is its pregiven role, given to it by the nature of the totality. Sweezy makes this point when he writes:

> the desire of the capitalist to expand the value under his control (to accumulate capital) springs from his special position in a particular form of organization of social production ... We see that the Marxian analysis relates capital accumulation to the specific historical form of capitalist production. (1970, pp. 80–1)

Similarly, Mandel writes 'The capitalist's aim is to accumulate capital, to capitalize surplus value' (1970a, p. 133). H.D. Dickinson, in an important article on the falling rate of profit, echoes this sentiment: 'There is an inherent tendency for capitalists to accumulate (or turn into new capital) a large proportion of the surplus-value that they appropriate' (1957, p. 120). Paul Zarembka makes this point emphatically as well. He writes that: 'The essence of capitalism is control over as much living labor power as possible – i.e., extending capitalist social relations as much as possible at each historical moment. We refer to this drive as the drive for the *accumulation of capital*' (1977, p. 11). David Yaffe links capitalism's inner essence, accumulation, with its telos: 'Capitalist production has as its aim and driving force the production of surplus-value as additional exchange value' (1973, p. 193).

It should be stressed what is not being argued here. It is not being argued that the capitalist enterprise is structurally enforced to accumulate due to the exigencies of capitalist competition. This belief that it is capitalist competition which drives accumulation and not the opposite, i.e. that accumulation drives capitalist competition, is a very common one in the Marxian literature. As will be argued in Chapter 3, this position is consistent with a microfoundations approach to understanding the laws of the social totality, rather than the 'holistic' approach being developed here. In contrast, the point being made here is that in the traditional debate over the TRPF, accumulation is understood to be the inner law of motion of capitalism whose logic is manifested in and through the capitalist enterprise. This point is important because there has been recently a considerable debate over the 'choice criteria' used by capitalists when deciding whether, and by how much, to accumulate, or whether or not to adopt a technical change.[18] A similar concern has been whether accumulation is characterized by a labor or a capital bias. These issues, which are relevant in the debate over the Okishio theorem, are not relevant ones in the traditional debate over the TRPF. Indeed, the Hegelian approach to totality does not allow these questions to even be posed, as its entry-point is that accumulation is the inner essence of the capitalist totality, and not the rationality of different capitalist choice criteria.

In a passage especially pertinent to this point, Marx refers to the relationship between accumulation and competition in the *Grundrisse* (1973) where he discusses the falling rate of profit. Referring to Adam Smith he writes:

> A. Smith's phrase is correct to the extent that only in competition – the action of capital on capital – are the inherent laws of capital, its tendencies, realized. But it is false in the sense in which he understands it, as if competition imposed laws on capital from the outside, laws not its own. Competition can permanently depress the rate of profit, if ... and insofar as a general and permanent fall of the rate of profit, having the force of

a law, is conceivable prior to competition and regardless of it. To try to explain the inner laws of capital simply as the results of competition means to concede that one does not understand them. (ibid., pp. 751–2)

For Marx, then, at least in the *Grundrisse,* accumulation is to be understood as existing prior to competition. Competition is a manifestation of capitalism's inner essence, accumulation. It is certainly not surprising that the above statement is found in the *Grundrisse* which is considered to be Marx's most Hegelian 'mature' work.[19]

Not only is capitalism's development driven by an inner law of motion, this law is also a contradictory one: accumulation drives capitalism through distinct phases or moments in a dialectical process. This contradictory process gives rise to a number of teleological interpretations about the laws of motion of capitalism and the role that the TRPF plays in capitalism's development.[20] The TRPF is one manifestation of capitalism's contradictory inner law of motion, accumulation. David Yaffe makes this point when he writes that:

> The general law of capitalist accumulation from the standpoint of capital (and the capitalist) represents itself 'on the surface of phenomena' as a tendency of the rate of profit to fall. This is not a mechanical or algebraic relation but the *expression of the contradictory nature of the accumulation process* from the standpoint of capital (1973, p. 199).

The issue of whether or not accumulation's contradictory development ensures a TRPF has been the object of longstanding debate. There has been no debate that capitalism's inner essence is accumulation. Instead, the issue of concern has been whether the law of the TRPF is a correct specification of capitalism's inner essence and teleological structure.

Indeed, various interpretations of the Marxian theory of the TRPF have each in different ways been understood as part of the teleological process of capitalist accumulation. There are three ways in which this has occurred in the literature: through theories of the business cycle, through theories of different stages of capitalism, and through the theory of the breakdown of capitalism.

Each of these teleological processes is based roughly on the following stylized logic. Capitalism is a totality driven by its inner essence, accumulation. The process of accumulation engenders contradictions such that this process will tend periodically to cease. This occurs because as accumulation progresses, the organic composition of capital rises and therefore the value rate of profit falls. The fall in the rate of profit subsequently stops or inhibits further accumulation. As accumulation slows, various forces come into play so that the process of accumulation can begin anew.[21]

This dynamic can be divided into three phases, each of which corresponds to a different moment of a dialectical process. The accumulation phase is the affirmation which eventually gives rise to its opposite, the crisis phase. The crisis phase is the negation of the accumulation phase. The crisis phase is only a transitory phase as the crisis gives rise to conditions such that this phase is transgressed. This transgression, or supersession begins the dialectical process of accumulation over again. This process is self-contained. While certain exogenous conditions might interfere with this process from time to time, the dialectic of accumulation–crisis–renewed accumulation will nevertheless reassert itself over time.

The three versions of this process found in the literature can be differentiated by the exact manner in which each dialectical phase is understood. However, an underlying dialectical logic is common to all three versions.

First, accumulation and the TRPF have been understood as a basis for a theory of the *business cycle* by a number of authors. Mario Cogoy writes that 'Marx sees his theory of the tendency of the rate of profit to fall in connection with the cyclical movement of capitalist production' (1973, p. 61). Maurice Dobb states in *Political Economy and Capitalism* that:

> It seems clear that Marx regarded this falling profit-rate tendency as an important underlying cause of periodic crises, as well as a factor shaping the long-term trend: as a fundamental reason why a process of accumulation and expansion would be self-defeating in its effects, and hence would inevitably suffer a relapse. (1945, p. 108)

For Dobb, a rise in the organic composition of capital was a result of the fall in the rate of profit due initially to a rise in wages. Dobb's logic clearly lays out the role of the TRPF as a theory of the business cycle. He argued that accumulation, during the boom phase of the business cycle, would give rise to an increase in wages as the reserve army of the unemployed was diminished as the demand for labor rose. Capitalists, in response to the increasing wages, adopt labor-saving techniques in an attempt to maintain profitability. As a result of this change in technique, the organic composition of capital will rise. For Dobb, any depressing effect on the rate of profit due to the tendency for the organic composition of capital to rise will be offset by a cheapening of constant capital and a rise in the rate of exploitation.[22] Insofar as these latter two counteracting tendencies lead to a rise in the rate of profit, a new phase of the accumulation process will be set in motion.

Here, then, the business cycle is understood teleologically. The accumulation process is understood to go through a dialectical process of boom, crisis and rejuvenation. Through all phases of the cycle capitalism's inner essence, accumulation, acts as the governor, creating the conditions for each phase to follow logically from the previous one.

Another teleological interpretation of the role of the TRPF in the accumulation process is one where the TRPF causes capitalism to move through various *stages* or *epochs*.[23] Sweezy has argued that during the period of competitive capitalism there is a tendency for the rate of profit to fall, but as capitalism progresses to a higher stage, monopoly capitalism, there is instead a tendency for the rate of profit to rise rather than fall. Sweezy writes:

> Marx's law of a falling tendency of the rate of profit was rooted in the conditions of nineteenth-century capitalism. But it must be added that it loses plausibility when applied to the fully mature capitalism that emerged in the twentieth century. (1981, p. 52)

During the period of competitive capitalism in the nineteenth century, Sweezy argues, the accumulation process was characterized by a transition from manufacture to machinofacture. This transition involves the replacement of hand-labor (manufacture) with that of machines (machinofacture) in the production process. It is reasonable, he asserts, to assume that the organic composition of capital rises sufficiently in this period to cause the rate of profit to fall. However, once the production process has been by and large mechanized it is no longer reasonable to assume that technical change will take the form of machines replacing labor. Indeed, technical change will now involve the substitution of more productive machines by less productive machines and the organic composition of capital will have a tendency to fall as simultaneously the rate of exploitation rises. The rate of profit will therefore have a tendency to rise rather than fall.

The fall in the rate of profit in competitive capitalism helps bring on capitalism's next stage, monopoly capitalism. As the profit rate falls some capitalist enterprises go out of business, or are bought up by competing enterprises. This process of centralization speeds up the tendency for capitalism in its mature stage to be monopolized. The competitive nature of capitalism is not diminished with the advent of monopoly capitalism however. There is still a tendency, indeed a necessity Sweezy argues, for capitalists to keep their costs as low as possible and innovate as often as possible. What has changed is the way in which accumulation manifests itself.

This changed manifestation of accumulation is most explicitly expressed by Sweezy and Paul Baran in their book *Monopoly Capital* (1975). There they write that as a result of monopolists' ability to keep prices high and costs low it is 'a law of monopoly capitalism that the surplus tends to rise both absolutely and relatively as the system develops' (1975, p. 80). They compare this law to the law of the TRPF and conclude that they have not done away with the law of the TRPF but have only recognized a new manifestation of the accumulation process which is appropriate in the monopoly stage of capitalism.

By substituting the law of rising surplus for the law of falling profit, we are therefore not rejecting or revising a time-honored theorem of political economy: we are simply taking account of the undoubted fact that the structure of the capitalist economy has undergone a fundamental change since the theorem was formulated. What is most essential about the structural change from competitive to monopoly capitalism finds its theoretical expression in this substitution. (ibid., p. 80)

The dialectical process involved here is one where each phase, or moment, of the dialectic is understood to be a particular stage of capitalism. Competitive capitalism is the affirmation of the dialectic. Embedded within competitive capitalism, however, are contradictions which lead to its negation and supersession. Capitalism's new affirmation, monopoly capitalism, begins a new dialectic which will eventuate in 'higher stages' of capitalism. Governing each stage of capitalism, however differently, is capitalism's inner law of motion, accumulation. It is accumulation which guides and structures the teleological development of capitalism.

A third form of teleology in the debate over the TRPF has been the belief that the TRPF would eventually lead to a *breakdown of capitalism*.[24] Capitalism is understood to be a distinct totality, a dialectic, whose existence is transitory. Capitalism's contradictory essence, accumulation, will eventually cease as the rate of profit falls ever lower. When this happens, a new dialectic, variously understood as socialism or communism, will emerge.

Those who hold to the TRPF as a theory of breakdown are often those who feel that the rate of profit must eventually fall as the production of surplus value has insurmountable limits. Mandel, for one, makes this link. He writes that 'The breakdown theory (zusammensbruch theorie) is based ultimately on this incapacity to overcome in the long run, the tendency of the rate of profit to fall, by way of increasing the rate of surplus value' (1970a, p. 168). Another supporter of the TRPF as a theory of breakdown is Rosdolsky, who also felt that the rate of profit would eventually fall as the amount of surplus value which capitalism could produce had unsurpassable limits and therefore capitalism could not continue (1977, pp. 376–82).

The TRPF as a theory of breakdown is often linked to political issues and strategies. In particular, the TRPF as a theory of breakdown is essential, for some, for an inevitably successful revolutionary politics to exist. David Yaffe (1973) and John Weeks (1982) are two who make this point.

Despite the differences between the business cycle, stages and breakdown versions of the theory of the TRPF all share a teleological understanding of capitalism's inner essence, accumulation, as manifested in the TRPF. Each posits an essentialist law of motion, driven by accumulation, and a succession of separate phases, stages or modes of production. The next section of this chapter will examine in detail the logical structure and contours of the debate over Marxian value theory and its impact on the theory of the TRPF.

The Traditional Debate over the TRPF – A Review

The traditional debate over the TRPF has been concerned primarily with the logical relationship between the Marxian value categories such as the organic composition of capital, the rate of exploitation and the value rate of profit. It has not been concerned with the question of whether or not accumulation is the law of motion of capitalism. The focus on the logical connections between the value categories reflects the fundamental shared methodological approach of all the participants in this debate. It is accepted by all that accumulation is capitalism's inner essence. Given this agreement, the issue of contention has then been over the way in which accumulation has been understood to affect the various Marxian value categories. As argued above, this focus on the logical connections between the Marxian value categories is in large part due to the rationalist epistemology underlying the Hegelian totality.

The Standard Argument

Consider a two-sector economy where one sector produces wage goods and the other sector produces capital goods. Assume that the wage goods and capital goods are homogeneous in each sector. Assume also that the real wage remains constant and that the rate of surplus value remains constant. Let the capital goods and wage goods be valued in terms of units of socially necessary abstract labor time. For simplicity, assume that the value of a commodity is equal in magnitude to its exchange value.

Define the following concepts.

$C = mK$ Total Constant Capital
$V = nbL$ Total Variable Capital

Where:

K = the total physical amount of the capital good in the economy
b = the physical amount of the wage good per hour of labor worked
L = total hours of labor worked in the economy
m = the unit value of the capital good
n = the unit value of the wage good

The value rate of profit for the economy as a whole can be defined as follows.

$r = S/(C + V)$ Value Rate of Profit

Where:

$S = L - V$ Total Surplus Value

As is well known, the value rate of profit can be rewritten in the following way.

$$r = S/(C + V)$$
$$= S/V/(C/V + 1)$$
$$= e/(k + 1)$$

Where:

$e = S/V$ Rate of Exploitation
$k = C/V$ Organic Composition of Capital

Given these definitions, the way in which Marx's theory of the TRPF is usually described is summarized nicely in Ronald Meek's influential 1960 *Science and Society* article.

> It follows logically from these definitions that if the rate of surplus value remains constant a rise in the organic composition of capital will bring about a fall in the rate of profit. And this, it is claimed, is what Marx said would actually happen with the development of capitalism over time. As capitalism developed, machinery would be more and more substituted for labor; the organic composition of capital would therefore tend to rise; and the rate of profit would therefore tend to fall. There were of course certain 'counteracting influences' ... which would retard the fall in the rate of profit. (ibid., p. 37)

The counteracting influences to which Meek referred and their effect on the value rate of profit have been the primary issues of the debate over the TRPF. In particular, the counteracting influences of the cheapening (in value terms) of constant capital and the production of relative surplus value have both received an enormous amount of attention in the literature. These two objections, and the responses to these objections, are important to focus on for two reasons. First, they have received the most discussion in the literature and are therefore highly influential. Second, they are objections which purport to be logically entailed by Marx's (or Meek's) argument as stated above. Furthermore, these objections are exactly the type that one would expect in a Hegelian context. Once the inner law of motion of the totality is discovered, in this case accumulation, then the next order of business is to draw out the *logical* implications of the discovered inner law. Theoretical debate therefore should be confined to the correctness or otherwise of the logical derivations made from the discovered fact that capitalism's essence is accumulation. Not coincidentally, this is the form which the vast majority of the traditional debate over the TRPF has taken.

Given the concern with the Hegelian aspects of the traditional debate over the TRPF, objections to the TRPF which take the form of the relaxation of certain specific assumptions will not be considered here. Thus, there will be no consideration of what happens to the value rate of profit if the real wage is allowed to vary or, alternatively, if capital and wage goods were to be denominated in terms of prices of production instead of values (or exchange values). These issues have only played a minor role in the traditional debate over the TRPF in any case.

Objection 1: Cheapening of Constant Capital

This objection concerns the issue of whether or not the organic composition of capital will rise as a result of accumulation. The form that this objection usually takes in the literature is to question whether *constant capital* actually rises with accumulation. It is generally accepted that as accumulation progresses capital goods will replace labor and therefore the technical composition of capital, defined as the ratio of capital goods to labor hours worked, will rise over time.[25] In the language of neoclassical economics, accumulation displays a labor-saving bias. This, however, does not necessarily imply that the organic composition of capital will rise as the organic composition of capital is a value magnitude.

To see that the organic composition of capital does not necessarily rise as the technical composition of capital rises, consider a 'rise' in the technical composition of capital in the capital goods sector only.[26] As the technical composition of producing capital rises, capital per unit of wage good rises. Assume that this in turn brings about an increase in the average productivity of labor. As the average productivity of labor rises, this entails a fall in the unit value of the produced capital good, as the average productivity of labor and the unit value are reciprocals of one another. The average productivity of labor is defined as total output divided by the total labor time needed to produce the output, and the unit value is the total labor-time divided by the total output.

It is entirely possible that while the mass of capital goods, K, increases with accumulation, the unit value of the capital goods could fall sufficiently so that the overall effect would be a fall instead of an increase in constant capital. Thus, accumulation could conceivably lower the organic composition of capital instead of increasing it.

This counteracting tendency to the TRPF has been remarked on extensively in the literature. For instance, Sweezy writes:

In physical terms it is certainly true that the amount of machinery and materials per worker has tended to grow at a very rapid rate for at least the last century and a half. But the organic composition of capital is a value expression; and, because of steadily rising labor productivity, the growth in the volume of machinery and materials per worker must not be regarded as an index of the change in the organic composition of capital. (1970, p. 103)

Despite the logical possibility that constant capital, and hence the organic composition of capital, could actually fall, Sweezy believes that empirically there is no doubt about the 'propriety in assuming a rising organic composition of capital' (ibid., p. 100).

Joan Robinson made a similar point in her *Essay on Marxian Economics*, where she wrote:

Inventions may, on balance, reduce capital cost per unit of output as much as labor cost, for they may improve the efficiency of labor in making machines as much as in working machines ... Technical progress may also reduce the period of turnover of capital goods. Chemical processes such as bleaching are speeded up, and the development of transport economizes the stocks which it is necessary to hold at each stage of production and marketing. This tends to reduce capital per man employed. Nevertheless, Marx takes the view that there is on balance a strong tendency for capital per man to increase as time goes by, and this assumption is a natural one to make. (1963, pp. 35–6)

Ernest Mandel in his influential *Marxist Economic Theory* stated that:

The growth in the organic composition of capital also works in the direction of lowering the prices of machines, and so of the value of constant capital in relation to variable capital, and thus opposes the tendency of the rate of profit to fall. (1970a, p. 168)

However, he went on to argue that while 'progress in productivity undoubtedly reduces the value of each unit of constant capital, this progress implies at the same time a considerable increase in the number of these units' (ibid., p. 168). Therefore, he concluded, constant capital does indeed rise over time.[27]

Roman Rosdolsky similarly defended an increase of the organic composition of capital. He did so on empirical grounds and argued that Marx explicitly considered such empirical evidence in his *Theories of Surplus Value* (1971). Rosdolsky claimed that there were two factors which Marx recognized would together ensure that the organic composition of capital would rise. First, while each individual machine would undoubtedly decrease in value, the production process would become more complex as a whole system of machines would replace the few machines previously employed in production. Second, the amount of raw materials used would greatly increase as workers became more productive (Rosdolsky, 1977, pp. 405–7).

Despite the logical possibility of a fall in constant capital, and along with it a fall in the organic composition of capital, it is perhaps safe to say that the overwhelming majority of opinion on this counteracting influence to the TRPF is that any decrease in the unit value of constant capital is swamped by the initial increase in the mass of capital goods.

The arguments, whether pro or contra the TRPF, of Sweezy, Robinson, Mandel and Rosdolsky, among others, are strangely incomplete. They correctly highlight the possibility that, as accumulation proceeds, constant capital may actually fall rather than rise due to the cheapening of its unit value. However, they fail to recognize the importance of the fact that the organic composition of capital is a *ratio* of constant to variable capital. Therefore it is the change in the ratio of the unit values, m/n, which must be considered in order to ascertain whether the organic composition of capital rises or falls with accumulation.[28]

In order to see the importance of this point consider the following analysis. Given that the technical composition of capital and the unit value of both the capital and wage goods move in opposite directions with accumulation, the effect of accumulation on the organic composition of capital can be seen in the following manner.

Let:

T = Technical Composition of Capital

and as above,

m = unit value of the capital good
n = unit value of the wage good

Assume that as accumulation proceeds over time the technical composition of capital rises. Assume also that the increase in the technical composition of capital increases the productivity of labor in both the wage good and the capital good sectors, and thus the unit values of both the wage good and the capital good fall. There is no presumption, however, that the increase in the productivity of labor is the same in each sector, and therefore no presumption that unit values in the capital and wage good sectors will fall at the same rate.

These assumptions can be expressed mathematically as follows:

$dT/dt > 0$
$dm/dt < 0$
$dn/dt < 0$

The organic composition of capital can be written now as:

$k = (m/n)T$

The rate of change of the organic composition of capital depends on the value of the following equation.

$\dot{k} = \dot{m} - \dot{n} + \dot{T}$

Where:

$\dot{k} = dk/dt(1/k)$
$\dot{m} = dm/dt(1/m)$
$\dot{n} = dn/dt(1/n)$
$\dot{T} = dT/dt(1/T)$

It can now be shown that the organic composition of capital will rise as accumulation proceeds over time under the following conditions. There are three cases to consider.

$\dot{k} > 0$ if either:

1 $\dot{n} > \dot{m}$. If $\dot{n} > \dot{m}$, then the decline in the unit value of the capital good, the numerator of the fraction m/n is smaller than the decline in the unit value of the wage good, the denominator in the same fraction. For this to occur the increase in the average product of labor in the wage good sector must be greater than the increase in the average product of labor in the capital good sector.

2 $\dot{m} > \dot{n}$ and $\dot{T} > \dot{m} - \dot{n}$. If $\dot{m} > \dot{n}$, then the fraction m/n will fall as the decrease in the numerator, m, will be greater than the decrease in the denominator, n. This will occur if the increase in the average product of labor in the capital good sector is greater than the increase in the average product of the wage good sector.

If the fraction m/n falls the organic composition of capital can still increase if the increased technical composition of capital is big enough to swamp the decrease in the ratio, m/n. This will occur when $\dot{T} > (\dot{m} - \dot{n})$.

3 $\dot{m} = \dot{n}$. If $\dot{m} = \dot{n}$, then the organic composition of capital will increase along with the technical composition. In fact, the increase in the organic composition of capital will exactly equal the increase in the technical composition of capital. That is, $\dot{k} = \dot{T}$ as $\dot{m} = \dot{n}$. The fall in the unit values, m and n, will be equal when accumulation is such that the rise in the average productivity of labor is equal in both the wage good and capital good sectors simultaneously.

These three cases exhaust the possibilites for changes in the organic composition of capital in the simple example of this section. If the capital goods and wage goods were heterogeneous, then the changes of the relative value magnitudes of all these goods would further complicate the analysis. The fundamental issue of the cheapening of unit values and its effect on the organic composition of capital would remain, however.

Objection 2: The Production of Relative Surplus value

As was pointed out above, the rise in the technical composition of capital due to accumulation will tend to increase the average product of labor in the capital goods sector. And, as was argued, it is equally true that a rise in the technical composition of capital will increase the productivity of labor in the wage goods sector. As a result, the unit value of the wage good will fall as accumulation proceeds. Assuming that the real wage remains fixed, as is generally done, then variable capital will fall with increased accumulation. A fall in variable capital will lead to an increase in the rate of exploitation. Marx defined in Chapter 12 of volume I of *Capital* the production of relative surplus value to be that rise in the rate of exploitation due to the cheapening of the wage good (1976, pp. 429–38). That is, the ratio between surplus labor time and necessary labor time will tend to rise, even as the length of the working day remains fixed.

To see this, rewrite the rate of exploitation in the following manner.

$$e = S/V$$
$$= (L - V)/V$$
$$= (L - nbL)/nbL$$
$$= (1 - nb)/nb$$

In order to calculate the effect on the rate of exploitation, e, as accumulation proceeds, and therefore the unit value, n, falls, it is necessary to calculate the derivative of e with respect to changes in n.

$$de/dn = (-bnb - b(1 - nb))/(nb)^2$$
$$= -b/(nb)^2$$

As b, the real wage, is positive, $de/dn < 0$. Thus, as n falls with accumulation, the rate of exploitation, e, rises.

If the rate of exploitation were to rise sufficiently so that the percentage increase in the rate of exploitation was greater than the percentage increase in the organic composition of capital (assuming it did increase), then the value rate of profit would rise, not fall, as a result of accumulation.

Sweezy, for one, believes that the increase in the rate of exploitation all but vitiates any claim that there is a tendency for the rate of profit to fall due to an increasing organic composition capital. For him, 'it would seem that we must regard the two variables as of roughly co-ordinate importance'(1970, p. 104). And, as a result, 'Marx's formulation of the law of the falling tendency of the rate of profit is not very convincing' (ibid.).

Joan Robinson makes a related point concerning the cheapening of the unit value of the wage good. She points out that the rate of exploitation can only remain constant if the real wage were to rise. This is because as the unit value of the wage good, n, falls with accumulation, variable capital will also tend to fall. Thus, unless the real wage rises, variable capital, V, will fall and the rate of exploitation, $e = S/V$, will rise. She concludes that there can be a guarantee of a falling rate of profit only if the real wage were to rise. However this, she claims correctly, goes against Marx's usual assumption of a constant real wage. She proceeds to reformulate Marx's law of the TRPF by incorporating the problem of effective demand, not an unsurprising theoretical tack given her strong association with Keynesian economics. She concludes:

> that Marx started off on a false scent when he supposed that it was possible to find a law of profits without taking account of the problem of effective demand, and that his explanation of the falling tendency of profits explains nothing at all. (1963, p. 42)

A number of authors have responded to this criticism by arguing that the increase in the rate of exploitation has definite unsurpassable limits while the potential increase in the organic composition of capital theoretically is unlimited. Therefore they conclude that the value rate of profit will eventually fall. For instance, Mandel writes that 'the increase in the rate of surplus value comes up against *absolute* limits (the impossibility of reducing necessary labor to zero), whereas there is no limit to the increase in the organic composition of capital' (1970a, pp. 167–8). Similarly, Rosdolsky states that Sweezy and Robinson 'overlook that the increase in the rate of profit secured by raising ... the exploitation of labour is no abstract procedure or arithmetical operation' (1977, p. 408). They forget that 'the surplus labour which a worker can perform has definite limits' (ibid., p. 408).

Ronald Meek argued this point through an example (Meek, 1967, pp. 141–2). Suppose, he wrote, that initially an economy has 20 workers who work twelve hours per day. Suppose the value of labor power per worker is eight hours. Thus, each worker produces four hours of surplus value per day, and 80 hours of surplus value are produced in the economy as a whole. Now suppose that accumulation is such that capital replaces labor and only three laborers are needed. Suppose further that the value of labor power for these workers is reduced to zero and that simultaneously the length of the working day is increased to a maximum of 24 hours. Clearly, this is the case of maximum exploitation. Meek wanted to show that even in this case not as much surplus value will be produced as previously. Each worker now produces 24 hours of surplus value and the economy as a whole only produces 72 hours of surplus value. Meek concluded that 'this illustration shows that on Marx's assumptions the possibility of compensating the effect of a rise in organic composition upon the rate of profit by a rise in the rate of surplus value (however caused) has certain impassable limits' (1967, p. 142).

There are serious problems with the above responses. Sweezy, for example, has called such arguments attempts 'to solve the problem (of a rising rate of exploitation, SC) by a pseudo-mathematical reasoning' (1981, p. 50). He points out that the total amount of necessary labor in an economy can tend to zero while all the other members of society could live off unemployment insurance paid out of the appropriated surplus value. This would mean that both the rate of exploitation and the organic composition of capital would tend to infinity as variable capital tends to zero.

Indeed, in Meek's example above, it is clear that after accumulation the rate of exploitation, $e = S/V$, will equal infinity, as $V = 0$. It seems that Mandel, Rosdolsky and Meek all overlooked the fact that the value rate of profit, $r = e/(k + 1)$, is a ratio of two ratios, e and $k + 1$. The value of these ratios depends on the value of the denominator, V, as well as the value of their numerators, S and C respectively.

The size of the value rate of profit as V approaches zero can be seen from the following example.

$$\lim_{v \to 0} r = \lim_{v \to 0} S/(C + V) = \lim_{v \to 0} (L - V)/(C + V) = L/C$$

The ratio, L/C, is the maximum rate of profit. That is, it is the rate of profit as variable capital approaches zero and the rate of exploitation approaches infinity. The maximum rate of profit has been used by a number of authors to defend the theory of a TRPF. Surprisingly, Okishio in a *Cambridge Journal of Economics* (1977) article argues that the maximum rate of profit will tend to fall over time as the capital–labor ratio increases. Okishio's analysis begins from the following mathematical truism.

$$r = S/(C + V) \leq S/C < L/C \quad \text{where } L = S + V$$

The ratio, L/C, is always strictly greater than the ratio, S/C, as any production will always require the use of some productive labor, no matter how small, and therefore variable capital, V, will always be greater than zero. Thus, L will always be strictly greater than S.

Now, as the capital–labor ratio, C/L, grows, L/C which is the maximum rate of profit will fall. As the maximum rate of profit falls, the value rate of profit, $S/(C + V)$, will be forced to fall as long as L/C approaches zero. If L/C does not approach zero, then the maximum rate of profit can fall asymptotically to some positive value, while the value rate of profit rises asymptotically to the same value.

The Hegelian Totality

It is also possible that the maximum rate of profit would approach zero as time approaches infinity. Thus, the 'actual' value rate of profit would be forced to fall only as time was very near infinity. The exact point where the value rate of profit would be squeezed would depend on the starting points and the relative slopes of the decline in the respective profit rates relative to time. Needless to say, the fact that the maximum rate of profit falls as the capital–labor ratio rises has not been a decisive argument against those who believe that there is no necessary reason for the TRPF as capitalism accumulates. As the maximum rate of profit might not squeeze the actual value rate of profit until some time in the distant future, there is no necessary tendency, it can be argued, for the value rate of profit to fall in the meantime.

There are many other particular issues which have been the subject of debate, only some of which can be covered here.[29] For instance, Ben Fine and Laurence Harris (1979) and Michael Lebowitz (1976) each claim, albeit in different ways, that all sides in the debate over the TRPF have misunderstood Marx's method. Fine and Harris argue that no one has understood correctly the relationship between the value composition of capital and the organic composition of capital, and therefore all have misunderstood Marx's law of the TRPF.

For Fine and Harris, Marx made a clear distinction between the organic and the value compositions of capital. They point out that, for Marx, the organic composition of capital directly mirrors the change in the technical composition of capital. The organic composition of capital is simply the value expression of the technical composition of capital. That is, the organic composition of capital abstracts from all changes in the unit values brought about by changes in the productivity of labor as the technical composition of capital changes. Thus, if the technical composition of capital were to rise, the organic composition of capital would necessarily also rise. On the other hand, the value composition of capital takes into consideration the productivity and distributional changes brought about by the initial change in the technical composition of capital, and therefore the changes in the unit values. These value categories capture for Fine and Harris the dialectical unfolding of capitalist accumulation. They write that 'Marx is separating two dialectically related processes: first, the increasing OCC associated with the rising TCC and productivity increase ... and second, the consequent reduction in the values of commodities associated with that productivity increase' (1979, p. 60).

For Fine and Harris, 'it follows tautologically that the rate of profit in value terms falls' (ibid., p. 62). But, they continue, this law should not be dismissed as a 'mere' tautology for it can already be seen that it is constructed on the basis of the concepts which come before it in *Capital*. It is the direct effect of the rising technical composition of capital; *and the necessity of that tendency itself follows from Marx's analysis of capital as self-expanding value*. (ibid., p. 62, my emphasis)

In other words, Marx's theory of the TRPF is an expression of capitalism's inner essence, accumulation.[30]

In a somewhat different direction, Lebowitz argues in a highly original and insightful article (1976) that the debate has overlooked the crucial fact that Marx introduced his theory of the TRPF first in volume III of *Capital*. Marx, Lebowitz argues, understands capital to be a totality, a unity between the spheres of production and circulation. As volume III presupposes the circulation conditions of volume II, Marx's value categories must be adjusted to take this into consideration. Lebowitz argues that the value categories in volume III are 'enriched' by the added determinations considered by Marx in volume II. In particular, the increasing cost of sales and attempts to lower turnover times must be included in any calculation of constant capital, and therefore any calculation, or theory, of the TRPF. These increased costs associated with the circulation of capital all but guarantee a TRPF for Lebowitz. To abstract from these costs is to misunderstand Marx's dialectical method, and therefore to misunderstand the dialectical unfolding of the accumulation process.

It is perhaps safe to say that the influence of Fine and Harris, and Lebowitz has not been a great one on the overall debate over the TRPF. That debate has been characterized, as argued in this section, by concern over the theoretical correctness of the two counteracting influences; the cheapening of constant capital and the production of relative surplus value. However, there can be no doubt that Fine and Harris, and Lebowitz should be located on the general terrain of the Hegelian totality on which the traditional debate has occurred.

Conclusion

By the mid-1970s this is more or less where the debate stood. As described in this chapter, the traditional debate over the TRPF, influenced as it was by the methodological framework of the Hegelian totality, had to a large extent played itself out. The different interpretations concerning the logical issues of Marxian value theory had been aired in full detail and few new insights were being put forward.

One could either reject Marx's theory of the falling rate of profit, as a determinate theory, as did Sweezy and Robinson, because of the supposed increase in the rate of exploitation. One could then adopt either theories of monopoly capitalism (Sweezy) or Keynesian demand insufficiencies (Robinson) as the basis for understanding the instabilities of capitalist crisis. Or one could argue theoretically (Meek, Rosdolsky, Yaffe, among others) that the TRPF was valid as a theory of capitalist crisis or empirically that the rate of profit had fallen if only the profit rate was calculated correctly (Gillman, Mandel).

At the same time that the traditional debate over the TRPF was reaching an impasse, new developments in Marxian theory were coming to the fore which would have dramatic implications for the debate over the TRPF in future years. On the one hand, following Sraffa's seminal work, *Production of Commodities by Means of Commodities* published in 1960, Marxian value theory was undergoing a fundamental challenge that reached its height in the late 1970s and early 1980s with Morishima's *Marx's Economics* (1973), Steedman's *Marx after Sraffa* (1977) and Roemer's *Analytical Foundations of Marxian Economic Theory* (1981). The argument of Morishima, Steedman and Roemer, although expressed differently, was that the classic concepts of Marxian value theory were incorrect and redundant.[31] The fundamental insights of Marx's theory of exploitation could be explained without explicit reference to value categories, and moreover reliance on these value categories gave incorrect results.[32] One such incorrect result, it was claimed, was Marx's theory of the TRPF. As will be explored in detail in the next chapter, this new critique of the traditional Marxian theory of the TRPF, builds on the Okishio theorem, named for an article by the Japanese Marxian economist Nobuo Okishio, first published in Japan in 1961. For some, the result of the Okishio theorem was so devastating to the law of the TRPF that it virtually wrote the 'obituary' for any further debate over this issue (van Parijs, 1980). The Okishio theorem, and the debate that it engendered, is the subject of the next chapter, and details of the argument will be presented there. Suffice it to say here that the argument of this book is not that the Okishio theorem convincingly disproved the Marxian theory of the TRPF, and thereby rendered moot any debate over it, but rather that it *displaced* the theoretical and methodological terrain on which the issues were debated.

As will be argued in some detail in the next chapter, this displacement occurred in part as a result of the change from a Marxian to a Sraffian value theory, but more importantly, perhaps, because of a change in the manner in which the social totality was conceived. This change in the nature of the social totality will be the focus of much of the next chapter. As already intimated in Chapter 1, the Hegelian totality which was ever present in the traditional debate over the TRPF would now be replaced with Cartesian totality which assumes that the parts of the social totality are determined independently and prior to the totality. The Cartesian totality is the mirror opposite of the Hegelian totality in this sense. In social theory, the Cartesian totality takes the form of methodological individualism or, alternatively, microfoundations. The 1970s and early 1980s was a period when the 'microfoundations revolution' took shape in mainstream macroeconomic theory.[33] It was also the time when those advocating such a position in Marxian theory began to gain influence, especially in the work of Roemer (1986) and Elster (1985).

Thus, as will be argued next, there was a shift in terrain on which the traditional debate over the TRPF occurred to a new Cartesian (or methodological individualist) terrain on which the debate over the Okishio theorem would and continues to occur. It is this debate and its methodological underpinnings with which the next chapter is concerned.

CHAPTER 3

The Debate over the Okishio Theorem and the Cartesian Totality

Nobuo Okishio's article 'Technical Change and the Rate of Profit', published in Japan in 1961 in the *Kobe University Economic Review*, set off one of the most intense debates in Marxian economics in the post-Second World War era.[1] At the heart of Okishio's article was a theoretical claim that had profound implications for analytical and political work the world over. Okishio's claim, or what has come to be known as the Okishio theorem, states that in a linear price of production model of the economy the general rate of profit will not fall as a result of technical change. For many, the Okishio theorem has completely disproved any tendency for the rate of profit to fall as capitalism grows and accumulation proceeds.[2] The Okishio theorem demonstrates logically, it is argued, that it is impossible for a 'rational' capitalist to adopt a technical change that will result in a falling general rate of profit.

For others, however, the Okishio theorem has thrown down the gauntlet of neoclassical methodology and reformist politics which must be expunged at all costs from Marxian economics. There can be no argument that on its own terms the Okishio theorem is logically and mathematically correct. Yet despite this, the debate over its result has engendered some of the fiercest polemics in Marxian economics in recent years. The purpose of this chapter is to sort out this recent debate and offer some new insight into the theoretical structure and positions of the various sides taken.

The tremendous impact which the Okishio theorem has had in the broader debate over the TRPF can be traced to reasons other than its political importance or logical coherence. In particular, the Okishio theorem is an instance in a larger debate occurring in Marxian theory in general, and Marxian economics in particular. That debate concerns the way in which the social totality is to be conceptualized, and the related issues of how causality is understood and the manner in which social explanations are to be formulated.

To foreshadow the major argument of this chapter, the Okishio theorem, and the debate surrounding it, takes place in the terrain of the *Cartesian totality,* as opposed to the traditional debate over the TRPF, which

Chapter 2 argued took place on the terrain of the Hegelian totality. In contrast to the holism of the Hegelian totality, the Cartesian totality begins from the ontological premise that its constituent parts exist prior to and independent from the totality. Indeed, the totality is assumed to be nothing more than the patterns which emerge from the interaction of its preconstituted parts. Associated with this notion of the Cartesian totality is a reductive form of causality, often referred to as a mechanistic or linear causality. Mechanistic causality is based on the assumption that the world can be divided into a succession of distinct moments of cause and effect. A cause must always occur prior to an effect, while an effect can always be reduced to the action of a preexisting cause. The goal of analysis then is to discover the basic causes, or parts, from which the distinct patterns of the totality can be deduced.

In social science the Cartesian totality has been associated with an approach to social explanation commonly referred to either as methodological individualism or, alternatively, the search for microfoundations to aggregate social behavior. Methodological individualism asserts that all explanations of social phenomena can, and should, be made in terms of the behavior of independently constituted individuals. That is, individuals are the social atoms from which all explanation of the social totality are to be deduced. Jon Elster, a Marxist philosopher, describes methodological individualism as 'the doctrine that all social phenomena – their structure and their change – are in principle explicable in ways that only involve individuals – their properties, their goals and their actions' (1985, p. 5). Elster goes on to state that methodological individualism is a form of reductionism, where society is reduced to individuals, just as molecules are reduced to atoms (ibid.).

It is often assumed along with the principle of methodological individualism that individuals act rationally. That is, individuals attempt to maximize their well-being (however defined) and act consistently in their attempts to do so. This approach to behavior is often labeled rational choice theory. It is not necessary, however, that methodological individualist explanations assume that individuals act according to the prescripts of rational choice theory.

As will be shown below, the Okishio theorem is based on a type of social explanation which is methodological individualist and, thus, is shaped by the Cartesian totality. The Cartesian totality gives rise to an irreducibly distinct Marxist social theory from that of the Marxist social theories based on the Hegelian totality. Thus the key terms of capitalist, economy and technical change that are employed in the Okishio theorem also take on an irreducibly distinct meaning and significance.[3] For instance, the capitalist enterprise (part) is reduced to the capitalist *qua* individual who is generally assumed to have the pregiven rationality of profit maximization. The economy (totality) is represented by the equilibrium of the linear price of production framework which is the result of the interaction of the profit maximizing capitalists (parts). In other words, the part (capitalist) exists prior to, and gives shape to, the totality (economy).

Not only is the Okishio theorem itself based on the Cartesian totality, but the presence of the Cartesian totality has slipped into, and left its stamp on, the arguments of even the most ardent critics of the Okishio theorem. Thus various Marxist theorists such as Anwar Shaikh (1978b, 1980), John Weeks (1982) and Pat Clawson (1983) all operate to varying degrees on the terrain of the Cartesian totality in their critiques of the Okishio theorem. Indeed, with the notable exceptions of Ben Fine (1982) and Ian Hunt (1983), most of the critics of the Okishio theorem operate on the terrain of the Cartesian totality. The issues of debate over the Okishio theorem — in particular what is the 'correct' behavioral assumption to make concerning individual capitalist choice — have then been profoundly different from those in the traditional debate over the TRPF. Indeed, the issues of concern in the traditional debate over the TRPF are nonissues, or nonsensical ones, in the debate over the Okishio theorem. Similarly, these issues of debate over the Okishio theorem were nonissues in the traditional debate as, in particular, the capitalist was assumed there to simply act out its inner essence, accumulation, which was given to it by the nature of the totality.

In effect, the debate over the Okishio theorem has occurred, and continues to occur, in the context of a fundamentally different Marxian theory from that of the traditional debate over the TRPF. As a result, what constitutes the appropriate modes of inference and method in each theory are in their core radically at odds with one another. Therefore it is not possible, as some have claimed (van Parijs, 1980), that the Okishio theorem has 'disproved' the TRPF, or in any absolute sense sent it to its grave. If an 'obituary' can be written about the TRPF and the debate over it, as van Parijs among others would like, then that obituary would have to take the form of 'old theories never die, they just slip into obscurity and disrepute'. If anything, then, the Okishio theorem has participated in the *displacement* of the traditional debate over the TRPF, but certainly not its disproof.

The Linear Price of Production Model of the Economy

Before discussing the Okishio theorem, and criticisms of it, in detail, it will be useful first to examine the linear price of production model of the economy on which both the Okishio theorem and the vast majority of the critiques of it are based. The linear price of production model is a paradigmatic Cartesian way of conceiving the workings of the overall economy. Indeed, this model of the economy can be conceived metaphorically as a machine whose outcome (general equilibrium) is the direct result of its prior and independently constituted parts.[4] To understand the workings of the machine (the economy) then, the parts must be identified and disembodied from the totality (again, the economy) and examined.

The linear price of production model is often referred to in the literature simply as the 'Sraffian model' following Sraffa's seminal 1960 *Production of Commodities by Means of Commodities*. There have been many subsequent formulations and developments of this model since Sraffa's original work and, as a result, a Sraffian, neoRicardian, or alternatively 'surplus product' school of thought has developed in economics that is distinct from both neoclassical and Marxian economics.[5]

The linear price of production model can be represented by the following vector of 'n' price of production equations.

$$\mathbf{p} = (1 + r)(\mathbf{pA} + \mathbf{pbL})$$

Where:

- A = the matrix of physical commodity inputs per unit output, where a_{ij} represents the amount of commodity i required to produce one unit of commodity j.
- L = the row vector of labor inputs per unit output.
- **b** = the column vector of commodities advanced per unit of labor; b_i represents the amount of commodity i consumed by a worker in return for an hour's labor time.
- **p** = the row vector of prices of production per unit of output.
- r = the general rate of profit.

The matrix, A, and the vectors, **b** and **L**, are data determined exogenously outside of the model. The law of one price is assumed to hold which implies that there is one and only one price of production for each distinct commodity. There are n sectors, or industries, producing the n commodity outputs. There is a single, uniform, economy-wide rate of profit due to the assumption of perfect competition. The assumption of perfect competition also guarantees that the hourly wage, **pb**, is equal across sectors.

There are n price equations in the model. However, there are n+1 variables to be determined, i.e. the n prices and the general rate of profit. Thus, the system is underdetermined. By normalizing one price to equal one, the system is determinate now with n − 1 relative prices and the general rate of profit. The solution to the n − 1 relative prices can be found by rewriting the price of production equations in the following manner:[6]

$$\mathbf{p} = (1 + r)(\mathbf{pM})$$

Where:

$$M = A + bL$$

Expressing this result in the context of the Cartesian totality as briefly outlined above, the equilibrium configuration of the $n-1$ prices of production and the general rate of profit is the totality whose existence depends on the prior specification of the parts A, **b**, **L**. Together, the equilibrium prices of production and the general rate of profit divide the social product into two segments: one which is used to replace the technical inputs and the real wage used up in production, and another that represents the surplus product which is to be apportioned equally between the sectors in the economy.

The role of the capitalist enterprise is generally overlooked in linear price of production models. There is a good reason for this; the effectiveness of the capitalist enterprise is reduced simply to a production process for each particular commodity. Indeed, the very concept of an active, decision-taking capitalist appears only implicitly in these models. Presumably, the capitalist is taking decisions about the relative profitability of different investment decisions and that is why there is assumed to be an equal rate of profit across sectors of the economy. *Mathematically*, of course, it is possible to simply pose by fiat an equal rate of profit across sectors. In essence, such a requirement simply constricts the number of variables in the model by limiting the potential profit rates from n to one. However, the assumption of profit maximization must be made in order for the equal-rate-of-profit-condition across sectors to make *economic* sense. That is, there must be some presumed rationale why resources would flow from low rate of returns to higher ones and thereby equalize the sectoral rates of profit.[7]

This subtle point is not often made in linear price of production of models, and need not technically be made, as pointed out, for the model to solve. It must be made, however, if the model is to be consistent with the requirements of a microfoundational approach.[8] John Roemer recognizes the importance of explicitly stating this behavioral assumption when he remarks that:

> Speaking of equilibrium makes no sense if one has not specified behavioral rules for the agents, in this case, the capitalists. In the Marxian system (as in others), capitalists seek to maximize profits. One should therefore derive the equal-profit-rate (EPR) price vector as a consequence of profit maximization on the parts of capitalists. (1981, p. 17)

Jon Elster makes the same point in defending the approach of methodological individualism. Using a linear price of production model, Elster shows how the macroeconomic result of an inverse relationship between wages and profits can be derived from microeconomic foundations. He asserts that 'The underlying postulate of an equal rate of profit in the consumption sector and the capital sector follows from the microeconomic postulate of profit maximization and the assumption of unrestrained competition, *and can be justified in no other way*' (his emphasis, 1983b, p. 112). Implicit, then, in linear price of production models of the economy is the assumption of a pregiven capitalist rationality of the maximization of profits. It is not clear, however, how decisions are actually to be made and profits maximized in such models as the capitalist enterprise never appears as a site of actual decision-making. In this sense, the capitalist of the linear price of production models, and *ipso facto*, in the Okishio models of technical change, can be understood as *expressing* the inner essence pregiven to it by the analyst. This inner essence is one which expresses the 'self-evident' human nature of what it means to be first, an individual (act rationally = maximize), and second, to act as a capitalist (maximize profits).

Thus, despite the tremendous differences in approach between the 'capitalist *qua* accumulator' of the traditional models of the TRPF and, as will be seen, the 'capitalist *qua* profit maximizer' of the Okishio models, they share a fundamental similarity. They both reduce the capitalist to a homogeneous conceptual category which acts out its given role. The object of theoretical discourse is, then, to deduce, i.e. trace out the logical implications of, the capitalist's predetermined action. In other words, despite the myriad differences between each approach, they share in common the commitment to a rationalist epistemology and the methodology of logical deduction which is often associated with such an epistemological stance.

However, by emphasizing this similarity, it is not meant to conflate the dramatic differences between their two respective conceptions of the economy. In particular, as mentioned, the linear price of production model conceives of the economy metaphorically as a machine, a Cartesian totality. The parts of the economy, therefore, exist prior to and independent from the subsequently constituted totality. The metaphor of economy as machine can be seen especially lucidly in John Roemer's reconceptualization of Marxian economics using set-theoretic mathematics common in modern, neoclassical general equilibrium models (Roemer, 1981). Roemer defines the concept of a Marxian equilibrium as 'A price vector **p** is a reproducible solution (RS) for the economy $\{A, \mathbf{L}; \mathbf{b}; \omega^1 \ldots \omega^n\}$ if ...' (ibid., p. 19). The terms are defined as above and the ω's are vectors of initial material endowments for each capitalist, one through n. Roemer goes on to list four conditions for a reproducible solution to exist: profit maximization, the economy can reproduce its inputs, the workers receive the subsistence wage and the initial endowments for the economy as a whole are sufficient to cover the input requirements for production.

Roemer shows that given these assumptions there exists a reproducible vector of prices and output levels for the economy. In other words, once the above-specified parts are assumed, a coherent totality will emerge. Roemer 'lays' out the parts of his economy in set notation, much like the parts to a model airplane are laid out prior to construction. The assumption of perfect competition is the glue which adheres the various parts – {A, L; b; ω^1 ... ω^n} and profit maximization – into the totality, or equilibrium configuration of the economy.

Changes in the linear price of production model are conceptualized as the movement from one equilibrium configuration to another. This notion of change is often referred to as comparative statics. Change is initiated when one part in the originally specified economy undergoes a transformation, or alternatively, a new part is added to it. For instance, if a technical improvement in the ith sector of the economy occurs such that more output could be produced with fewer inputs, this would imply that the unit coefficients in that sector would fall. The equilibrium configuration of the economy would be perturbed as the new parts (the changed input coefficients) will not now 'fit together' (the innovating sector will earn an above average profit rate). However, assuming that the technical change does not violate any of the technical assumptions of the model, a new equilibrium configuration of prices and a general rate of profit consistent with the changed parts will emerge. In other words, a new totality will result from the newly constituted parts which will replace the previously constituted one. It is important to note that the changed input coefficients which resulted from the technical improvement did not come about endogenously. Neither the totality, nor any of the other parts, caused the technical change. Rather, the changed input coefficients were the result of some unspecified exogenous change. That is to say, the technical change occurred first, and only subsequently, and contingent upon that change, did the original totality disintegrate, and subsequently did a new totality emerge as a result of the other parts mechanically responding to the initial change. This is, of course, an example of the mechanical and linear causality that is associated with modes of explanation which are commonly deployed in social analysis shaped by the Cartesian totality.

The linear price of production model is commonly used by those advocates and critics alike of the Okishio theorem. As a result, the debate over the Okishio theorem has occurred, and continues to occur, almost exclusively on the terrain of the Cartesian totality. In this sense, the continued popularity of the Cartesian terrain in the debate over the TRPF is an indicator of the displacement of the traditional debate over the TRPF by the Okishio debate. The next two sections of this chapter will focus directly on the Okishio theorem and its critics in order to show more precisely and dramatically the Cartesian influence on this important Marxian debate.

The Okishio Theorem

The non-falling rate of profit result of the Okishio theorem depends critically on its use of a Sraffian approach to value theory and methodological individualism, and *per force*, the Cartesian totality. The methodological individualist approach has recently become so popular that both the proponents and opponents of the Okishio theorem often base their positions on the terrain of the Cartesian totality.

The Okishio theorem is based on the following explicit assumptions.

1. The economy is characterized by a linear price of production model with a Leontief input matrix (the matrix, A, in the previous section).
2. There is no fixed capital; only circulating capital.
3. There are no non-produced means of production.
4. Real wages are fixed.

The first assumption implies that the economy is perfectly competitive so that the profit rate, the wage rate and the price of production of each commodity is uniform across the economy. Assumptions 2–3 are technical assumptions which have been relaxed in various extensions of the Okishio theorem.

The Okishio theorem also makes a behavioral assumption concerning the choice of technique by a capitalist. It is assumed that a capitalist will introduce a new technique of production if and only if it raises its rate of profit at the going set of prices. Technical changes of this sort are often labeled *viable technical changes*. It is this assumption around which much of the debate over the Okishio theorem has occurred. It is also this assumption which puts the Okishio theorem squarely in the methodological individualist framework.

Given the above assumptions, the economic logic of the Okishio theorem is often described schematically as follows. Suppose a capitalist discovers a viable technical change and adopts it. At the going set of prices the capitalist will be able to earn super profits, i.e. above average profits. In an effort to capture more of the market the innovating capitalist will lower its output price. In turn, this initial price reduction of the innovating capitalist will translate into input price reductions for the capitalists in all the other sectors of the economy. They will in turn adjust their output prices, which will affect all the input prices of the other capitalists, including the capitalist who initially innovated. What the Okishio theorem proves is that once this complicated process of price adjustment has worked itself out, and a new set of equilibrium prices of production and a new general rate of profit emerge, then the new profit rate will be greater than the previous one, assuming that the technical change occurred in a basic industry. A basic industry is one whose commodity output enters either directly or indirectly as an input to the production of every other commodity in the economy. If the original innovation occurred in a non-basic industry, then the profit rate will remain the same. In any case, the profit rate cannot fall as a result of a viable technical change.

The mathematical result and logic of the Okishio theorem is impeccable once the above assumptions are granted.[9] Its appeal is due in part to two factors. First, the capitalist is simply assumed to be myopically self-interested. The innovating capitalist only has to calculate the effect of a potential technical change on its own rate of profit at the going set of prices. The capitalist does not have to be able to predict the effect of adopting the technical change on its future profitability or the future set of prices in the economy.[10] Second, the Okishio theorem provides a resolution to the complicated and seemingly unending process of price-cutting and adjustment described above by showing that this process will eventually arrive at a new equilibrium and that the new profit rate cannot have fallen.

That the Okishio theorem is based on a methodological individualism and the Cartesian totality is a straightforward extension of the linear price of production model of the economy. The equilibrium of a linear price of production of the economy is a totality derived from the interaction of the preexisting parts, A, L and b. The Okishio theorem asserts that a change in a given equilibrium configuration of the economy (totality) to another as the result of a technical change can never lower the general rate of profit. The initiator of the technical change is the capitalist who obeys the specified viability condition. That is, the economy or totality adjusts from one equilibrium to another due to the originating action of an individual capitalist. The economy responds to individuals and not *vice versa*. This is, of course, a methodological individualist explanation of the effect of technical change on the rate of profit.

Critiques of the Okishio Theorem

If the number of journal pages devoted to a theoretical issue can be considered an appropriate index for its importance, then the Okishio theorem was one of the most important issues of Marxian economics in the 1970s and 1980s. In large part the amount of attention that has been directed towards the Okishio theorem has been due to its political importance. If, as is argued by some, the Okishio theorem is correct, and therefore there is no inherent TRPF as capitalism accumulates, then there is also no objective necessity for a socialist transition (Yaffe, 1973). In an article discussing the theory of the TRPF in general, and the Okishio theorem in particular, John Weeks emphasized the political importance of the debate over the TRPF when he claimed:

the debate over the tendency for the rate of profit to fall relates directly to key questions of political strategy – the role of the wage struggle and 'economistic' demands, possible divisions within the capitalist class and their significance, and class alliances for the overthrow of capitalism and the construction of socialism. (1982, pp. 62–3)

For Weeks acceptance of the Okishio theorem implied a reformist and economistic political practice, its rejection a revolutionary and transformative politics. The debate over the Okishio theorem, however, is not only the locus of these political concerns, it is also an important site of theoretical struggle within Marxian theory in general, and Marxian economics in particular. It is this theoretical struggle which is of concern here, and therefore this section will not directly comment on the political importance of the Okishio theorem.

Virtually all of the critiques of the Okishio theorem are made explicitly within the context of the Cartesian totality, or at least adopt terminology and theoretical strategies consistent with the Cartesian approach. In fact, the Cartesian totality has become such an accepted commonplace in this debate that Ian Hunt, one of those who does not accept the Cartesian foundation of the Okishio theorem, does so with noticeable trepidation and apologia. He writes 'At the risk of sounding terribly "metaphysical", accumulation should not be viewed primarily as the product of capitalists' decisions' (1983, p. 140). Instead accumulation, he continues, 'is fundamentally an *expression* of capital's tendency to expand value without limit ... Capital accumulates with a rising organic composition of capital because it thereby *immanently* resolves at a certain level of the articulation of the accumulation process a contradiction between accumulation and profits' (ibid., p. 140, my emphasis). Another 'non-Cartesian' critic, Ben Fine, is less contrite. His argument against those supporters of the Okishio theorem is that they do not accurately capture the dynamic and contradictory nature of the capitalist accumulation process. It is only through the correct use of Marx's value categories of the value composition of capital, the organic composition of capital and the value rate of profit that this process can be understood. The falling rate of profit then is a necessary implication of the capitalist accumulation process (1982, pp. 110–27).

The Okishio theorem is based on a number of restrictive technical assumptions such as no fixed capital, no non-produced means of production, and a constant real wage. There have been a variety of critiques, as well as extensions, made of the Okishio theorem by relaxing various of these assumptions. Perhaps the one which has drawn the most critical attention has been the assumption of no fixed capital. A number of theorists have argued that a viable, cost-reducing technical change must, at the very least on an intuitive level, involve an increase or change in machinery, and therefore a change in fixed capital. Anwar Shaikh (1978b) and John Weeks (1982) have attempted to argue that the presence of fixed capital vitiates the Okishio result. John Roemer was one of the first to extend the Okishio theorem in a formal model which explicitly incorporated fixed capital. He did so first in a von Neumann model assuming an infinite life for fixed capital and no joint production (1978), and later also in a von Neumann model in which fixed capital, differential turnover times, and joint products are taken into account (1980). In both articles he showed under appropriate assumptions that viable technical changes would not result in a falling rate of profit. On that basis, he concluded that the Okishio result was robust enough to incorporate fixed capital into its ambit. Jose Alberro and Joseph Persky have similarly shown that even in a simple two sector model a viable technical change will lead to a rising rate of profit, even while assuming the presence of fixed capital (1979). Takeshi Nakatani (1980) cites an article which Okishio published in Japanese in 1963 where he extended his original theorem by assuming fixed capital. In contrast to these results Neri Salvadori (1981) showed through the use of an example that, in a model where fixed capital is understood to be a joint product, technological change can lower the rate of profit in the short run. However, he argued, this implies nothing about the secular movement of the rate of profit.

Bill Gibson and Hadi Esfahani proved, assuming the presence of non-produced means of production, i.e. land, that there is a possibility for a falling rate of profit, even in the Okishio context. They demonstrated that if a change in technique is such that two production processes of different efficiencies are used on the same quality of land, and thereby intensive rent is earned, 'it is quite a trivial matter to construct a feasible technology such that the rate of profit falls and rent rises' (1983, p. 99). Taking a different direction, David Laibman has argued that rather than holding real wages constant it is better to hold the rate of exploitation constant. The latter, he claimed, better reflects the notion of class struggle neutrality that has been implicitly made in analyses of technical change on the rate of profit, than does the assumption of a constant real wage. Given this assumption of a constant rate of exploitation and therefore a variable real wage, he showed that viable technical changes can indeed lead to falling rates of profit (1982).

What is remarkable about these criticisms and extensions is that they remain within the context of the Cartesian totality, and therefore contest the Okishio theorem on its own turf, so to speak. All of the above criticisms are based on the linear price of production models consistent with the Cartesian approaches. Salvadori, for instance, proclaims that his analysis shows 'the possibility ... of a contradiction between capitalist motivation at the microeconomic level and the macroeconomic effects of capitalists' decisions' (1981, p. 65). In a similar vein, Laibman concludes that:

We have seen that, given the preferred embodiment of class struggle neutrality in a constant rate of exploitation, there are definite conditions, consistent with capitalist 'micro-rationality', in which a rising organic composition of capital and a falling rate of profit can occur. (1982, p. 104)

While these critiques are squarely based in the context of methodological individualism, they do not contest the particular form of capitalist rationality. With only slight variations all assume that capitalists are rational, profit maximizing individuals as encoded by Okishio's viability condition. They all share a basic *modus operandi* of critique; a relaxation of one of the 'technical' assumptions of the model such as fixed capital, no non-produced means of production or a constant real wage.

There have, however, been a number of critiques which confront directly the profit maximizing behavior of capitalists (Shaikh, 1978b; Weeks, 1982; Clawson, 1983). These critiques fit more uneasily in the Cartesian world as each in part attributes to accumulation a fundamental role in driving capitalist development. However, capitalist competition acts as a filtering process which screens certain types of innovations and individual capitalists are understood to have particular rationalities, for example maximizing their survival probabilities. Insofar as accumulation is seen as a fundamental driving force of capitalist development, these authors are consistent with the Hegelian approach described in Chapter 2.[11] However, to the extent that these authors give a fundamental role to capitalist rationality, they fall within the Cartesian approach. This tension between the Hegelian and the Cartesian approaches is most dramatically played out in a series of papers by Anwar Shaikh, whose influential article on Maurice Dobb in the *Cambridge Journal of Economics* in 1978 initiated the major debate over the Okishio theorem in the 1980s. Shaikh has been one of the most persistent and hostile critics of Sraffian economics in general, and the Okishio theorem in particular. Shaikh's article shows how even the most ardent of critics of the Okishio theorem has in part given way to the terrain of the Cartesian totality and bases his critique on its foundation.

Shaikh's major claim in his article is that the Okishio theorem's assumption of no fixed capital is incompatible with its assumption concerning the nature of capitalist competition. For Okishio, capitalist competition requires that capitalists introduce cost-reducing technical changes on pain of elimination from the market due to the presumed, aggressive, price-cutting behavior of their competitors. Shaikh agrees with Okishio on this point. However, he argues that the way in which unit costs must be lowered, which therefore allows a capitalist to lower its output price, requires investment in ever larger units of fixed capital. In other words, a condition of existence for the reduction of current, or circulating capital costs is an increase in the capitalist's fixed costs.

Shaikh recognizes that some may argue that a cost-minimizing capitalist could introduce capital-saving technical changes (i.e. labor-intensive innovations) which would then not require any investment in fixed capital. Such innovations will not occur, Shaikh argues, because capitalists will only introduce labor-saving technical changes owing to the ever present struggle between workers and capitalists over the conditions of the labor process. Thus capitalist technical change will of necessity be of a type that increases the roundaboutness of production and therefore the amount of fixed capital employed.

The recognition that investments in fixed capital are needed in order to lower current unit costs allows Shaikh to define two rates of return. On the one hand, he defines the *profit margin* to be the ratio of profit in relation to capital used up in production (circulating capital). On the other, he defines the *profit rate* as the ratio of profit to capital advanced. The profit margin is the ratio of two flows, while the profit rate is the ratio of a flow to a stock (i.e. the stock of new investment capital). Shaikh now demonstrates through an example that for a capitalist who minimizes current costs of production, thereby satisfying the Okishio viability criterion, it is indeed possible for the profit rate to fall even though the profit margin rises. Thus, Shaikh claims that 'Rather than being incompatible, these two results are simply different aspects of the same contradictory process' (1978b, p. 244). This contradictory process (of accumulation) which is reflected in the rise of the profit margin and the fall of the profit rate is reflective of Shaikh's Hegelian methodology. The Cartesian influence is brought out as Shaikh recognizes that he must also argue why a rational capitalist would ever adopt a technical change which would lower its profit rate. Are not capitalists assumed to be rational, profit maximizers? Shaikh identifies this position with what he calls the 'choice of technique' school associated with a number of Sraffian economists such as Ian Steedman, Pierangelo Garegnani, and others. These economists, he asserts, assume that capitalists can 'choose' the optimal technique of production available to them. In contrast, Shaikh believes that the exigencies of capitalist competition always enforce a particular behavior on every capitalist, a behavior which requires capitalists to adopt the least costly technique available.[12]

Now with two rates of return there are seemingly two criteria for the adoption of new technical change. Shaikh labels the *optimality criterion* that criterion for the adoption of a new technique of production based on increases in the profit rate. He calls the *competitive criterion* that criterion based on reductions in current costs of production which will in turn raise the profit margin. Shaikh claims that the optimality criterion is the one consistent with a neoclassical or Sraffian description of a harmonious perfect competition where capitalists can make Pareto superior choices that improve their profitability while harming no one else. It is the competitive criterion, however, which governs the choice of technique if one assumes a 'true' description of capitalist competition. For Shaikh a true description of capitalist competition would recognize that:

> competition is not a game. It is a war, in which the big devour the small, and the strong happily crush the weak. The laws which competition executes in turn frequently execute many of the competitors. And the principle weapon of this warfare is the reduction of production costs, for every such reduction enables a capitalist to lower his prices and drive his competitors out of the field without simultaneously ruining himself. (1978b, pp. 204–1)

It is this second notion of competition which Shaikh adopts. Capitalists on pain of elimination, must adopt techniques of production, which allow them to lower their current unit costs and therefore their prices. Not to do so threatens that they will be driven from the market into bankruptcy, as one's competitors will surely adopt such cost-reducing techniques and lower their prices. Thus, argues Shaikh, the apparent choice of technique is only chimerical. Capitalists must obey the competitive criterion when adopting new techniques of production. This requires ever greater investments in fixed capital in an effort to lower current unit costs which, in turn, implies that the profit rate will fall (due to the increased fixed costs) and the profit margin will rise (due to the falling unit costs). Thus Marx's theory of the TRPF is vindicated once the 'true' nature of capitalist competition is understood.

Despite Shaikh's concerted attack on the 'choice of technique' school, and his advocacy of a structurally enforced capitalist behavior, his analysis falls within the ambit of the Cartesian totality. Instead of basing his analysis on the rational choice of profit maximizing capitalists, Shaikh assumes alternatively that capitalists are greedy, cutthroat competitors. Although this assumption differs from the 'choice of technique' school, Shaikh nevertheless assumes that all capitalists act on the basis of this pregiven motive. That is, capitalists are understood to be homogeneous social atoms just as in the Sraffian model of the economy on which the Okishio theorem is based. True enough, the outcome of capitalist rationality in Shaikh's analysis is an economy where the profit rate is lower than before the changes in technique occurred. However, the economy, the totality, is understood as the resulting configuration of the interactions of the preconstituted capitalists, and in this sense Shaikh's analysis falls within the Cartesian approach of the theorems proved by Okishio, Roemer, Bowles and others.

This form of equilibrium configuration is the result of what in game theory is called a Prisoner's Dilemma game.[13] Pat Clawson, in an article defending the theory of the TRPF, describes capitalist competition in a similar manner. He writes that 'each capitalist is always forced to accumulate at the most rapid pace he can or else he soon goes out of business' (1983, p. 108). He goes on to claim that in a world of cutthroat competition 'Firms face the prisoners' dilemma: each must accumulate in the hope of beating the others with a better product or lower cost, yet the net result is that they are each worse off than if they colluded' (ibid., p. 109). The Prisoner's Dilemma game assumes that each participant, here capitalist, has the same rationality before they begin the game. That is to say, all play by the same rules. The outcome of the game, the totality, is the pattern which emerges after the players act out their pregiven rationality.[14] Thus, Clawson, as well as Shaikh, levels his critique at the Okishio theorem squarely within the terrain of the Cartesian totality.

This point, with a couple of notable exceptions, has generally gone unnoticed in the literature. In an article defending the use of a micro-foundations approach in Marxian economics, Philippe van Parijs concludes that even

> Shaikh's attempt to vindicate the theory of the falling rate of profit, however vociferous against neoclassical Marxism in the narrow sense, must be viewed as a variety of neoclassical Marxism ... Indeed, the most fascinating feature of Shaikh's attempt was precisely that the alternative foundation he proposed for the alleged tendency rested on the rational behavior of individual capitalists. (1983, p. 119)

Ben Fine similarly recognizes that Shaikh has changed terrain from the traditional debate over the TRPF. He writes that despite the fact that Shaikh is critical of Okishio 'it is important to emphasize that it [Shaikh's argument] rests within its tradition and does not depart from it ... This is because Shaikh, like the Okishians, proceeds to determine the economy from the behavior of individual capitalists' (1982, p. 125). Fine's recognition that Shaikh determines the economy from the behavior of capitalists, and not *vice versa*, is once again a recognition of the changed terrain of the debate from the Hegelian to the Cartesian totality.

It should be stressed here that while van Parijs and Fine both understand that Shaikh, Clawson and others are squarely within the terrain of the Cartesian totality, they nevertheless 'see' only the opposed approaches of the Hegelian and Cartesian totalities. On the one hand, Fine rejects the Cartesian terrain in favor of the Hegelian (1982, pp. 117–21). Van Parijs, on the other hand, accepts the Cartesian terrain on which the Okishio theorem is based as a theoretical improvement. He writes, for instance, that:

> the specification of microfoundations offers the only promising path ...
> It is only by explicating the nature of the mechanisms which they

presuppose that we can hope to fit a wide array of disconnected explanations and theories into a common framework ... it is an essential precondition if one is to provide a proof of such a tendency, instead of comfortably begging the question. (1983, pp. 120–1)

For whatever reasons, it seems that van Parijs cannot imagine an alternative way in which to avoid the teleology and functionalism of the Hegelian totality without falling into the reductionism and structural determinism of the Cartesian totality. In the following chapter, I will develop just such an alternative, one which avoids the teleology and determinism of both the Hegelian and Cartesian totalities.

Shaikh's article subsequently spawned a lively debate that was squarely within the microfoundations approach to social theory. Ian Steedman (1980) contested Shaikh's distinction between the competitive and optimality criteria, arguing that the so-called choice of technique school in fact supported Shaikh's competitive criterion as the basis for the adoption of a technical change. Takeshi Nakatani (1980) claimed that the optimality criterion must in fact be the correct criterion and offered a numerical example to demonstrate this. Philip Armstrong and Andrew Glyn (1980) argued that in an oligopolistic industry the least-cost criterion does not necessarily apply, as a capitalist could use his capital to purchase financial capital and thereby remain competitive. Michael Bleaney (1980) claimed that one should take into account the fallibility of capitalists' expectations and the effect that this would have on the rate of profit. John Roemer (1979) and Philippe van Parijs (1980) both claimed that Shaikh did not adequately take into account the role of the interest rate in capitalist investment decisions. All of these critics focused their analysis on the purported motivation of the capitalist. In other words, all contested how the basic pregiven rationality of the capitalist is to be understood. None, however, contested whether one should question the microfoundations approach.

Shaikh's response to his critics was to reemphasize his understanding of capitalist competition based on a different microfoundations from that which his critics variously put forth. In his response (1980) Shaikh also pointed out that concepts are contained within particular theoretical constructs, and are not strictly comparable from one discourse to another. He wrote that:

In recent years we have witnessed a tremendous revival of Marxian economics. It has gained adherents rapidly, and after long years of stagnation it has begun to incorporate into it many of the powerful new tools developed in the interim. But these tools never come free of charge; without exception, they are developed in the framework of an orthodox system of concepts, and *unless consciously examined for their hidden premises*, these premises become smuggled in with the techniques themselves. This is all the more so since orthodox economics tends to present itself as merely a series of applications of a set of objective and neutral tools. (1980, p. 76)

Shaikh's point about being self-conscious concerning the origin of one's theoretical tools is well taken. It has been one of the major points I have made, in this and the previous chapter, with respect to the different Hegelian and Cartesian approaches to social totality. In Shaikh's case, he is certainly well aware of the need for theoretical self-consciousness concerning the use of such 'neoclassical' tools as constrained optimization mathematics and equilibrium systems. However, it appears that he is not fully aware of the effectivity of the Cartesian totality on his analysis of the TRPF and the Okishio theorem.

This chapter has thus far outlined the linear price of production model, the Okishio theorem and the debate which has occurred over its validity. The major argument that has been developed throughout is that there has been a shift in the terrain on which the Marxian debate over the falling rate of profit has taken place. The effect of this shift in terrain, towards the Cartesian totality, has been accepted by the vast majority of critics of the Okishio theorem, and as a result the traditional debate over the TRPF has been displaced by this new one over the Okishio theorem. As this shift has recurred in a number of areas of Marxian theory it is important to detail the philosophical foundations and history of this approach in order to establish what is at stake in this shift, and to show exactly how profound a shift in theoretical approach it is. Consequently, the next two sections of this chapter will examine the ontological and methodological foundations of the Cartesian totality and the microfoundational approach to social theory. Finally, it will be shown how this approach has increasingly influenced and transformed Marxian theory, forming as a result a new Marxian theory based on the microfoundations and Cartesian approaches to social theory.

The Cartesian Totality

The Cartesian totality is an assertion about the ontological structure of the world. According to the Cartesian totality any totality, whether animate, inanimate or social, is composed of a set of basic elements or atoms which exist prior to and independent from the totality. The totality then is nothing more than the resulting configuration of the patterns of interaction of its independently constituted parts.

The Cartesian totality is the ontological foundation on which numerous social theories are based. These theories of society generally go under the rubric of 'individualism' as they assume that society is nothing more than the patterns that emerge from the interaction of independently constituted individuals. Associated with this ontological assumption is the claim that the proper form of an explanation should be methodological individualism. That is, all societal facts should be explained on the basis of the pregiven dispositions and beliefs of individuals.

The reductionist approach of the Cartesian totality goes back to the Greeks and their atomistic theory of the universe. Democritus, who lived between 460 BC and 370 BC, was perhaps the earliest atomist. He believed that the physical world consisted of the patterns of a few basic atoms. For Democritus even the soul was composed of nothing more than atoms. At a slightly later date, Epicurus similarly claimed that all matter, and man too, was composed in the end of nothing more than a few basic atomic elements.

It was Descartes, however, who stamped indelibly on modern thought the idea that the world was ultimately decomposable into a set of independently constituted parts, and therefore that the 'proper' method for understanding reality was to discover, and then analyze one by one, its pre-existing parts. Descartes outlined his approach in Part V of his *Discourse on Method* (1956) where he likened the inanimate and animate world to a machine. The machine metaphor has come to dominate Western thought (Lewontin, Rose and Kamin, 1984, p. 45). A machine is a totality whose parts can be disarticulated and examined separately. Each part maintains its essential integrity despite being disconnected from the totality, the machine. The parts can then be reassembled and the machine, which is nothing more than the summation of the parts, reconstituted.

In part two of the *Discourse on Method* Descartes discussed the principle rules of his method. These rules require that one dissect any problem of understanding into its most basic and evidently true elements. Then one can build up a *knowledge* of the problem in an orderly fashion from the basic elements. This method is the foundation and guiding principle on which methodological individualism has been constructed.

It is perhaps in the natural sciences that the Cartesian totality has had the greatest influence. Beginning with Newtonian physics of the eighteenth and nineteenth centuries, and continuing through Einstein's search for the field equations to which all areas of physics could be reduced, physics, and *ipso facto* all science, sought to discover the few basic foundation stones on which the natural world was constructed. In the field of biology biochemists have attempted to reduce the functioning of an organism to its most basic molecular structure.[15] In evolutionary biology the controversial but rapidly growing field of sociobiology has attempted to show that the evolution of animal species and human societies can be reduced to the genetic structures of the organisms or individuals of which they are composed.[16]

It has been against these reductionist approaches of science in general, and the genetic reductionism of sociobiology in particular, that Richard Lewontin, Steven Rose, Leon Kamin, Richard Levins, Stephen Jay Gould and others have been able to clarify the ontological structure of the traditional approach to science.[17] They have shown that natural science, and therefore much of social science, rests on the Cartesian totality. As Richard Levins and Richard Lewontin are particularly clear and insightful in their description of what they call Cartesian reductionism, it is worth quoting them at length.

Levins and Lewontin describe in detail the ontological structure of the Cartesian totality in their fascinating book *The Dialectical Biologist*.[18] They write there that:

> In the Cartesian world, that is, the world as a clock, phenomena are the consequences of the coming together of individual atomistic bits, each with its own intrinsic properties, determining the system as a whole. Lines of causality run from part to whole, from atom to molecule, from molecule to organism, from organism to collectivity. As in society, so in all of nature, the part is ontologically prior to the whole. We may question whether in the interaction new properties arise, whether the 'whole may be more than the sum of its parts', but this famous epistemological problem comes into existence only because we begin with an ontological commitment to the Cartesian priority of part over whole ... But Cartesianism is more than simply a method of investigation; it is a commitment to how things really are. (1985, p. 2)[19]

In their concluding chapter on 'dialectics' they list four ontological commitments of the Cartesian totality which have been 'The dominant mode of analysis of the physical and biological world and by extension the social world, as the social "sciences" have come into being' (ibid., p. 269). These four points are:

1 There is a natural set of units or parts of which any whole system is made.
2 These units are homogeneous within themselves, at least insofar as they affect the whole of which they are the parts.
3 The parts are ontologically prior to the whole; that is, the parts exist in isolation and come together to make wholes. The parts have intrinsic properties, which they possess in isolation and which they lend to the whole. In the simplest cases the whole is nothing but the sum of its parts; more complex cases allow for interactions of the parts to produce added properties of the whole.
4 Causes are separate from effects, causes being the properties of subjects, and effects the properties of objects. (ibid., p. 269)

These four characteristics then 'put their stamp on the process of creating knowledge' (ibid., p. 269). The first three points are statements about the ontological structure of the Cartesian totality. The fourth point concerns the nature of causality, which is to be understood in a mechanistic or linear sense. The common philosophical metaphor of the billiard ball is an appropriate description of this form of causality. When the cue ball is struck it sets in motion a chain reaction as the other billiard balls are struck by the cue ball. The cue ball is the cause and the others are the effects. In order to understand the consequent motion of the billiard balls one need only examine the initial conditions, or ultimate cause, i.e. the striking of the cue ball, along with the independently existing environment in which the billiard balls interact.

The first three points are especially important in methodological individualist explanations in general, and the Okishio theorem in particular. To anticipate the argument below, these three points imply the following critical features of methodological individualism (and the Okishio theorem). First, the natural set of units is the individual (the capitalist). Second, individuals are the basic building blocks of social analysis. They are the primitives of social explanation, the element to which all else is reduced and from which no further reduction is possible. In the Okishio theorem, for instance, the activity of the capitalist enterprise is reduced to a function of the will of the capitalist. An accurate description of the desires and volitions of the individual capitalists is the basis from which all explanation about the enterprise and economy is derived. All capitalists are assumed to be alike insofar as they all share the same rationality and goals (profit maximization).[20] The third point implies that individuals have intrinsic properties which affect the social totality but are not in turn affected by it. Usually it is assumed that individuals have embedded within their 'psyches' the pregiven desire and capacity to maximize the attainment of some end or goal. It is not explained or examined from where these goals and the norm of maximization come. They are given to the analysis. For example, as was shown above, the Okishio theorem assumes that capitalists wish to maximize profits and from this pregiven motivation all else can be derived (assuming certain technical details and perfect competition).

These characteristic four points of the Cartesian totality can be found in different ways in the work of various theorists advocating methodological individualism and the social analyses based on it. The Cartesian totality creates a fundamentally different conceptual framework in which to evaluate the issue of technical change and its effect on the rate of profit from that which is created by the Hegelian totality. Consequently, the issues of concern in each debate must be evaluated on their own terms and not on the basis of the other.

Methodological Individualism

Methodological individualism is a form of explanation commonly deployed in the social sciences. Its fundamental assertion is that all social explanations are incomplete, and therefore incorrect, unless and until they can be derived from the behavior of independently constituted individuals. Individuals are understood to be the 'atoms' of more complex social institutions such as classes, governments, enterprises, whole societies and so on. These complex social institutions are to be explained in terms of preexisting individuals, not according to their inner logic or some transcendental metaphysic. That is, the characteristics and properties of social institutions are to be deduced from the beliefs and dispositions of individuals, and not *vice versa*. Methodological individualism, then, is a form of social explanation based squarely on the ontological structure of the Cartesian totality. Social totalities are nothing more than the patterns of atomistic individuals colliding in social space, and therefore social explanations should be made in terms of these atomistic individuals and the social patterns which they create.

The use of methodological individualist explanations of social institutions has a long history. Hobbes was one of the first to claim that society should be understood as the unintended result of individual actions. Steven Lukes in his book *Individualism* (nd) explained that Hobbes held 'that "it is necessary that we know the things that are to be compounded before we can know the whole compound" for "everything is best understood by its constitutive causes," the causes of the social compound being Hobbesian men' (p. 110). Hobbes, of course, felt that society would be characterized by a 'war of all against all' which would require the presence of a state in order to mitigate against potential social disruptions.[21] Bernard Mandeville's *The Fable of the Bees* (1962) was perhaps the first systematic application of 'invisible hand' explanations in social theories. Mandeville gave many examples of how evil social consequences could result from the good intentions of individuals, as well as how good social consequences may result from evil intentioned behavior. Adam Smith in the *Wealth of Nations* (1965) introduced the invisible hand metaphor into economics. He argued that independently constituted, selfish individuals acting for their own benefit would lead to a socially optimal outcome. This insight has been subsequently formalized in neoclassical economics as the first theorem of welfare economics: an economy in competitive general equilibrium will be Pareto optimal (Arrow and Hahn, 1971).[22]

Fritz Machlup claimed that Schumpeter was the first to use the term methodological individualism (1951, p. 100). In coining this phrase, Schumpeter was concerned to make the distinction between what he called political individualism and methodological individualism. He wrote that while they shared a similar name they

> have nothing in common. The former starts from general premises, such as that freedom contributes more than anything else to the progress of

mankind and to the common welfare, and proceeds to a series of practical assertions; the latter does nothing of the sort, asserts nothing and has no particular premises. It means merely that in the description of certain economic processes one had better begin with the actions of individuals. (quoted in Machlup, ibid., pp. 100–10)

Schumpeter is surely mistaken on at least one count. Methodological individualism does indeed assert something and is unequivocally based on certain specific premises. In particular, methodological individualism depends on the ontological structure of the Cartesian totality and all that implies as described in the previous section.

The distinction which Schumpeter made between political and methodological individualism has not always been made in the literature. Friedrich Hayek and Karl Popper launched an all-out attack in the 1940s in the journal *Economica* against what has variously been called methodological holism, methodological collectivism or historicism. Hayek published an extended three part article entitled 'Scientism and the Study of Society' (1942–44). In the concluding essay of his 'trilogy' Hayek considered 'certain practical attitudes which spring from the theoretical views already discussed' (1944, p. 27). These practical attitudes concerned the belief that only consciously and purposefully directed actions will suffice to regulate societies. Hayek saw such attitudes as resulting from a holistic way of thinking and the fact that social scientists lacked 'a composite theory of social phenomena ... [which can] grasp how the independent action of many men can produce coherent wholes, persistent structures of relationships which serve important human purposes without having been designed for that end' (ibid., p. 27).[23] Popper continued this frontal attack on holistic social theory in a series of articles in *Economica* published in 1944 and 1945.

Popper's articles were subsequently published as a book entitled *The Poverty of Historicism* (1957). The main object of this book was to argue against holistic forms of social explanation and for methodological individualism. Popper, as did Hayek, stressed the link which he saw between different forms of social explanation and their political consequences, and in particular between holism and oppressive regimes. Indeed, Popper made this link abundantly clear in the dedication to his book: 'In memory of the countless men and women of all creeds or nations or races who fell victims to the fascist and communist belief in Inexorable Laws of Historical Destiny' (ibid.). For Popper, the way to avoid these unfortunate political consequences was to recognize that:

> the task of social theory is to construct and analyze our sociological models carefully in descriptive or nominalist terms, that is to say, *in terms of individuals*, of their attitudes, expectations, relations, etc. – a postulate which may be called 'methodological individualism'. (ibid., p. 136)

Popper continued this line of attack on holism and advocacy for individualistic modes of explanation in his influential book *The Open Society and Its Enemies* (1950), where he extensively critiqued both Plato and Marx. It may fairly be said that after Hayek and Popper holistic social theory, if not completely defeated, was in hasty retreat. Certainly in mainstream neoclassical economics there can be no question that after Hayek and Popper methodological individualist explanations rapidly became the dominant and only legitimately scientific ones. For example, Keynes' *General Theory* (1964), in which he attempted to develop a 'macroeconomics' not based on the individualist precepts of the 'Classical' economics of Pigou, was rapidly transformed into what is now known as the 'neoclassical synthesis', where Keynes' concern over the possibility of equilibrium unemployment is given rational microfoundations (Dow, 1985 and Brown-Collier and Bausor, 1988). Also, witness the proofs by Arrow and Debreu (1954), Debreu (1959) and McKenzie (1959) in the 1950s of the existence of a Pareto efficient general equilibrium set of prices, and the subsequent dominance in the economics profession of the techniques of general equilibrium theory.[24]

The connection between political and methodological individualism which Hayek and Popper propounded gave way in the 1950s and 1960s to a debate over the role of *reduction* in social explanations. In a series of papers J. W. N. Watkins (1952, 1955, 1957) and Joseph Agassi (1960) put forth, and defended, methodological individualism as the proper manner in which to frame social explanations. These proponents of methodological individualism were criticized by Maurice Mandelbaum (1955, 1957), Ernest Gellner (1960), L. J. Goldstein (1956, 1958) and May Brodbeck (1958), among others, for an over-reliance on reduction as the basis for explanation. The central concern of this debate was whether theories about social entities could and should be reduced to theories that began from predicates of individual behavior. This debate was concerned with two separate issues. First, there was the ontological concern of whether society and/or social institutions consisted fundamentally of pregiven individuals, and their dispositions and beliefs, or whether social entities were supervenient to the individuals who in part composed them. Second, there was the cognitive question of how society, however ontologically constituted, was to be understood and socially explained.

The individualist answer to the first issue was that social institutions, societies, etc. are ultimately composed of individuals. That is, social totalities are nothing more than collections, or patterns, of individual behavior. This claim is what Steven Lukes has called 'Truistic Social Atomism' (1968, p. 120), and as such, is for him a banal proposition, true 'in virtue of the meaning of words' (ibid.). This claim, however, is by no means a banal truism. It is based on a particular ontological assumption about the nature of the world, the Cartesian totality, which is distinct, but no more or less a 'true' or accurate description of social reality than is the Hegelian totality, and has provided the theoretical framework for important debates in the history of social and economic theory as described above.

The second issue concerned the presentation of social explanation. Harold Kincaid in an article entitled 'Reduction, Explanation, and Individualism' writes that the methodological individualist is making the following type of reductionist claims concerning the cognitive superiority of individualist social theories.

1. social theory referring to social entities, events, etc., is reducible to theory or theories referring to individuals;
2. such reduction is perhaps not possible now but is *in principle* possible; and
3. reduction requires lawlike co-extensionality between the primitive predicates of social theory and some predicate in the reducing theory. (1986, p. 494)

These three principles have been, and still are, held by most methodological individualists as the guiding principles of 'good' social explanations, as well as by most economists. Indeed as Kincaid points out the attempt by economists 'to provide microfoundations for macroeconomics is a reductionist program in the traditional sense' (ibid., pp. 494–5).

Perhaps the most extensive statement of the methodological individualist 'manifesto' was given relatively early on by Watkins in 1957. He combined in the following statement both the ontological commitment to individualism, and hence the Cartesian totality, as well as the cognitive commitment to methodological individualist social explanations. For these reasons it is worth quoting Watkins at length.

> According to this principle, the ultimate constituents of the social world are individual people who act more or less appropriately in the light of their dispositions and understanding of their situation. Every complex social situation, institution, or event is the result of a particular configuration of individuals, their dispositions, situations, beliefs, and physical resources and environment. There may be unfinished or half-way explanations of large-scale phenomena (say, inflation) in terms of other large-scale phenomena (say, full employment); but we shall not have arrived at rock-bottom explanations of such large-scale phenomena until we have deduced an account of them from statements about the dispositions, beliefs, resources, and interrelations of individuals. (The individuals may remain anonymous and only typical dispositions, etc., may be attributed to them.) (1957, pp. 105–6)

There are five important attributes of methodological individualism which can be extracted from this quotation. These attributes are related in a fairly direct manner to the characteristics of the Cartesian theoretical program as described by Levins and Lewontin above. These attributes are:

1   *Ontological individualism*: 'the ultimate constituents of the world are individuals'
2   *Pregiven rationality*: 'people who act more or less appropriately in the light of their dispositions and understanding of their situation'.
3   *Homogeneity*: 'The individuals may remain anonymous and only typical dispositions, etc., may be attributed to them.'
4   *Reductionist explanation*: 'There may be unfinished or half-way explanations of large-scale phenomena (say, inflation) in terms of other large-scale phenomena (say, full employment); but we shall not have arrived at rock-bottom explanations of such large-scale phenomena until we have deduced an account of them from statements about the dispositions, beliefs, resources, and interrelations of individuals.'
5   *Totality as configuration of parts*: 'Every complex social situation, institution, or event is the result of a particular configuration of individuals.'

These five principles prescribe the format that methodological individualist explanations normally take. For instance, with regard to the discussion above concerning the Okishio theorem, it was shown that the Okishio theorem is constructed in part through a methodological individualist social explanation. The capitalist is the basic social atom of the Okishio model. Indeed, the capitalist enterprise is nothing more than an expression of the capitalist's pregiven rationality, understood to be the maximization of profits. All capitalists are assumed to share in this rationality, each is 'representative' of the conceptual category, capitalist, and therefore each is indistinguishable from one another. The capitalist is in essence just one of the interchangeable parts comprising the machine-like economy. Thus, in effect, one need only analyze the motives and beliefs of a randomly selected capitalist in order to understand the essence of its being. The totality is the equilibrium configuration which emerges from the interaction of the pre-existing, rationally constituted capitalists.[25] The properties of this equilibrium are to be deduced from the behavior of the capitalists, and not *vice versa*. A change in one of the parts, such as a technical change, will lead to a new totality as the parts (capitalists) interact and configure a new totality (equilibrium). The Okishio theorem, then, is a paradigmatic example of methodological individualism and, *per force*, the Cartesian totality.

In recent years the debate over methodological individualism has recurred in two disparate areas of intellectual concern. On the one hand, methodological individualism has been the subject of some interest in the 'applied' philosophy journals. A sample of these articles would include Richard Miller in the *Philosophy of Science* (1978), Patrick Burman in *Philosophy of Social Science* (1979), D. H. Mellor in *Philosophy* (1982), David Levy in *Economics and Philosophy* (1985) and Harold Kincaid in *Philosophy of Science* (1986). These articles have been by and large concerned with the rather technical discussion of the appropriateness of the use of reduction in social explanation.

On the other hand, there has been a growing group of theorists over the last 15 years who have explicitly advocated the use of methodological individualism in Marxian theory. Indeed, one could argue that beginning with Sraffa in 1960 and the subsequent integration of Sraffian, or neo-Ricardian, value theory into Marxian economics by Morishima (1973) and Steedman (1977), among others, that there has been implicitly a microfoundations approach present in Marxian economics. However, it was not until John Roemer (1979, 1981, 1982a) and Jon Elster (1982, 1983b, 1985) that a concerted attempt was made to develop Marxism on the explicit basis of methodological individualism.

Methodological Individualism and Marxian Theory

Over the last 15 years or so, there has been a growing number of Marxian theorists who have advocated that Marxism should adopt methodological individualism. This trend has given rise to a school of Marxist thought which has been variously referred to as – 'analytical' (Roemer, 1986), 'neoclassical' (van Parijs, 1983), 'game-theoretic' (Lash and Urry, 1984), or 'rational choice' (Hindess, 1984; Carling, 1986) – Marxism. The most common term used to describe the Marxian methodological individualist approach is simply analytical Marxism, as that is the nomenclature adopted by its two most ardent proponents, Jon Elster and John Roemer. While it is true that most of the participants in the debate over the Okishio theorem predate this trend, the mode of argument used in the Okishio debate has in fact been based, as was argued above, on the methodological individualist approach, and for this reason it will be useful to discuss some of the major reasons why analytical Marxists advocate that Marxism adopt methodological individualism.

As described above, methodological individualism has had a long history, going back to Hobbes, through the work of Hayek and Popper, and into the debates of the 1950s and 1960s. This history seems to have had little effect on the Marxist application of methodological individualism, as there are few if any references to its existence by the analytical Marxists.[26] This may be due to the fact that while the 'bourgeois debate' over methodological individualism was explicitly over the role of reduction in theory, those

Marxists who have recently advocated a methodological individualist approach generally do so in order to oppose the functionalist and teleological tendencies within much of Marxian theory. This is certainly the starting point from which Jon Elster (1982) and John Roemer (1981) have based their advocacy of methodological individualism.

In his 1982 *Theory and Society* article, Elster attacked the functionalism and teleology which he saw in many Marxist analyses of social institutions. He wrote that 'By assimilating the principles of functionalist sociology, reinforced by the Hegelian tradition, Marxist social analysis has acquired an apparently powerful theory that in fact encourages lazy and frictionless thinking' (1982, p. 453). The cause of this lazy and frictionless thinking for Elster was the failure by Marxists to provide specific *mechanisms* for their theories of the development and/or persistence of the social institutions of capitalism. For instance, he insisted that Marxists must explain exactly how workers decide to join together and form a class, or how exactly a particular state policy is functional for the reproduction of the bourgeoisie. Elster claimed that 'without a firm knowledge about the mechanisms that operate at the individual level, the grand Marxist claims about macrostructures and long-term change are condemned to remain at the level of speculation' (ibid., p. 454). In order to provide such a mechanism, Marxism should adopt methodological individualism and that, in turn, 'leads to a search for a microfoundations of Marxist social theory' (ibid., p. 454).

John Roemer, an economist, has also been one of the most ardent supporters of a microfoundations for Marxian theory. His book *The Analytical Foundations of Marxian Economics* (1981) is a re-evaluation of many of the most debated issues in Marxian economics. Roemer employs a set-theoretic mathematics commonly used in neoclassical general equilibrium theory and explicitly advocates a microfoundations approach to the issues he analyzes. For instance, concerning the question of the nature of technical change in capitalism, Roemer contrasts the micro to the macro approaches. He writes that 'The *microfoundations* approach consists in deriving the aggregate behavior of an economy as a consequence of the actions of individuals, who are postulated to behave in some specified way' (ibid., p. 7). He then points out that 'This micro approach is different from a macro approach, which might say: We postulate that technical change takes the form of an increasing aggregate organic composition of capital' (ibid., p. 7). As with Elster, Roemer advocates the microfoundations approach in order to avoid much of the functionalism of Marxian arguments. As an example of this method, Roemer suggests 'that one theorem of Marxism is a "microfoundations of class" analysis' (ibid., p. 8). Indeed, in his later book, *A General Theory of Exploitation and Class* (1982a), Roemer proceeds to provide game-theoretic, microfoundations for a variety of different forms of exploitation and class formations.

Both Elster and Roemer mean by methodological individualism, or microfoundations, a specific form of reductionist social explanation.[27] Roemer offers a definition fully consistent with the approach of the Cartesian totality: 'Methodological individualism is the deductive method: it attempts to deduce historical observations from basic postulates on individual behavior that are sufficiently fundamental to be considered self-evident' (1982a, p. 514). In other words, beginning with the reduction of society to the self-evident truth of homogeneous individuals (i.e. individuals act rationally), one then deduces (the inverse of reduce) the history of society from its preconstituted social atoms. Elster offers perhaps the clearest definition of methodological individualism in the Marxist literature.

> By this [methodological individualism] I mean the doctrine that all social phenomena – their structure and their change – are in principle explicable in ways that only involve individuals – their properties, their goals, their beliefs and their actions. Methodological individualism thus conceived is a form of reductionism. To go from social institutions and aggregate patterns of behavior to individuals is the same kind of operation as going from cells to molecules. (1985, p. 5)

It is difficult to imagine a more straightforward description than this of a mode of social explanation which is based on the Cartesian totality. Methodological individualism, for Elster, involves primarily two factors. First, all explanations should be reduced to their social atoms, individuals. Second, individual action should be based on intentional explanation. The key aspect of intentional explanation is 'the specification of the goal – the future state of affairs for the sake of which the action is undertaken' (ibid., p. 8). Intentional explanation, then, is a form of teleological explanation.[28] Actions taken by individuals are purposive, directed towards the attainment of an end or goal. However, Elster avoids the 'cosmological' teleology – where all aspects of society are driven by a single goal – of Hegel and others by insisting that the social totality first be reduced to its constituent individuals. Thus, instead of one single teleological law of motion which subsumes all of society as its effects, as in Hegelian Marxism, Elster's Marxism implies a different teleological action for as many individuals as there are in society. Society is literally the outcome that emerges as these teleologically constructed social atoms collide (interact) in social space.

Elster points out that intentional explanation does not necessarily imply rational choice theory. Rational choice explanations are a subset of intentional choice. Such explanations assume that individuals maximize, i.e. adopt, the best available means to attain their goals, and/or that they act consistently (transitively).[29] It is equally true that not all intentional explanations, or for that matter rational explanations, assume selfish behavior. Intentional and rational explanations can be based on the assumption of altruism, incontinence or behavior based on commitment.[30] However, actual analyses and formal models of social or economic situations are, almost without exception, based on the assumption of egoistical rational behavior. Elster employs this approach in his book *Making Sense of Marx* (1985) as well as in his game theoretic examples in his articles (1982, 1986). Similarly, the models used to prove or rebut the Okishio theorem all assume selfish, rational behavior on the part of capitalists.

What reasons have analytical Marxists given for the enthusiastic manner in which they have embraced methodological individualism? I have already explained how Elster and Roemer adopted methodological individualism in order, in their view, to avoid the functionalism and teleology of much of traditional Marxian theory. However, this cannot constitute a sufficient reason for adopting the microfoundations approach, as many other Marxists before them such as Adorno, Horkheimer, Althusser, Hindess and Hirst, and Resnick and Wolff, have also rejected functionalism but have not consequently turned to methodological individualism for salvation.

On one level, some analytical Marxists see methodological individualism as the obviously, exclusively, correct approach for social science. That Marxist theorists have hitherto not commonly used methodological individualism as the cornerstone of their analyses is testament, it is argued, to the Hegelian legacy which unfortunately is still running as an undercurrent through Marxism.[31] In response to a series of articles critical of his recent book *Making Sense of Marx* Elster states with some exasperation that he is 'frankly, disappointed that this issue should have such a central place in the contributions. I regard methodological individualism as trivially true, worth stating only because, triviality notwithstanding, it was regularly violated by Marx' (1986, pp. 66–7).[32] Similarly, Roemer takes methodological individualism as self-evident. He asks rhetorically why one should need to provide class analysis with a deductive basis. His answer, succinctly put, is: 'In part, because the question poses itself' (1982b, p. 519). That is, it is such a well-established scientific procedure, how could one possibly question its appropriateness?

Elster also provides a rationale for methodological individualism based on a defense of reductionism. For Elster, 'If the goal of science is to *explain by means of laws*, there is need to reduce the time-span between explanans and explanandum – between cause and effect – as much as possible, in order to avoid spurious explanations' (1985, p. 5). That is, scientific explanation should constantly seek to explain as many steps as possible in the causal chain between the initial and end events. In terms of the billiard ball metaphor mentioned above, a methodological individualist explanation would attempt to describe all the collisions between balls, and between balls and the sidebanks, etc. that occurred from the initial striking of the cue ball to the eventual sinking of the billiard ball in the desired pocket. Not to do so would be tantamount to explaining the sinking of the billiard ball in terms of God's will, or as the teleological result of some predesigned plan.

Applied to the social world, Elster's rationale for methodological individualism requires that social outcomes be explained on the basis of individual agency. For instance, rather than explaining 'accumulation' as necessarily taking the form of an increasing organic composition of capital because that is a reflection of the inner nature of capitalism or the structural exigencies of capitalist growth, 'technical change' (note the subtle, but important, change in terms) instead should be explained as reflecting the rational choice behavior of individual capitalist firms. And, as a result, Elster claims that 'Capitalist entrepreneurs are *agents* in the genuinely active sense. They cannot be reduced to mere place-holders in the capitalist system of production' (ibid., p. 13). The appeal to agency is a common theme running through the analytical Marxist approach.[33] As Alan Carling, in a review of what he calls 'Rational Choice Marxism' concludes, 'It seems possible to sum up this whole change of perspective in one phrase: the reinstatement of the subject' (1986, p. 25).[34]

Carling's remark points to the earlier debates in the 1960s and 1970s over humanism. In an attempt to avoid the political problems which some Marxists saw in a necessary connection between 'Stalinisms–holisms–structuralisms', there was considerable support for developing a theoretical–humanist Marxism which saw the 'subject' as the prime mover (essence) of history instead of the forces and relations of production which drove the Hegelian totality of traditional Marxism (Althusser, 1979). Today, as Carling, Elster and Roemer point out, there is similarly a reemphasis on the 'subject', but now for reasons of theoretical correctness rather than political correctness. One wonders how strict this distinction between political and theoretical humanism really is.[35]

Elster's and others' insistence on choice and agency, however, belies a structural determinism present in their formal models of society in general and the economy in particular. In these models an individual, for example a capitalist, is given a particular prescribed behavior, not by the inner nature of the social totality, but rather by its structural location in the model. For instance when Elster writes that capitalist production and 'Also, the choice of technique ... must be guided by profit maximizing considerations' (1985, p. 12), he is not making an innocent statement. He is, in fact, asserting that *all* capitalists should be understood to behave this way. Elster reduces capitalist behavior in two ways here. First, the capitalist is assumed to act according to the norm of maximization, i.e. rationally. Second, the rational behavior of the capitalist is assumed to be directed to the goal of profit. Let me stress this point again; *all* capitalists in the model are assumed to obey the *norm* of maximization with the *goal* of profit in mind. To be a capitalist is to be a profit maximizer. The various political and cultural aspects of the capitalist *qua* individual, and the myriad differences of financial position, political influence, product identification, etc. between and among different capitalists, do not matter in Elster's or any other of these microfoundation models of the economy and/or society. That is, capitalists are assumed to be identical or homogeneous by virtue of their structural location in the model. Their inner nature may not be a reflection of some pregiven totality perhaps, but it is just as pregiven, given by the rationality of the theorist who invented the capitalist and the model in which it operates. It should be added here that the behavior attributed to capitalists by the theorist is often couched in terms of *self-evident* truths about human nature. That is, each and every capitalist seeks to maximize profits *because* they are capitalists (structural determination), *and because* it is only 'natural' that capitalists want to earn as much profit as possible (self-evident human nature).

This point concerning the structural determination of individual behavior has also been made by Barry Hindess. He points out that:

> The construction of rational choice models requires not only that actors are rational ... but also that all actors within certain categories are rational in essentially the same way – for example, that all entrepreneurs are profit maximizers in a sense that is similarly defined for all entrepreneurs, that political parties are vote-maximizers, that individuals are characterized by preference sets with similar mathematical structures, and so on. What is at issue here is a kind of structural determination of actors' thought processes, at least in the sense that the stylized forms of calculation employed by actors in the model are given by the social categories to which they belong. (1984, pp. 262–3)

The structural determinism of individual agents in methodological individualist models of society has led some advocates of a broad microfoundations approach to reject the formal models of Elster, Roemer, *et al.* Adam Przeworski is a sympathetic critic of Elster and Roemer and would consider himself one of the members of the analytical Marxist school. Yet he is bothered by the homogeneity and structural determination implicit in the approach of Elster and Roemer. He finds Elster's programmatic statement of methodological individualism 'barren' (1985, p. 400). However, he claims that 'the critique of Marxism offered by methodological individualism is irrefutable and salutary, but the ontological assumptions of the rational-choice framework – in particular, the assumption of undifferentiated, unchanging, and unrelated "individuals" – are untenable' (ibid., p. 381). For Przeworski, 'while any theory of history must have microfoundations, the theory of individual action must contain more contextual information than the present paradigm of rational choice admits' (ibid., p. 381). Przeworski believes that game theory promises a solution to the 'structureless' models of methodological individualism, a solution which can potentially capture the interaction of the individual with its environment.

Andrew Levine, Elliot Sober and Erik Olin Wright (1987) make a similar point. They claim that it is possible to advocate a microfoundations approach to social theory that 'does not require a commitment to methodological individualism' (ibid., p. 83). They correctly see no need to equate microfoundational analysis with rational choice models. They point out that 'There are many other possible kinds of microfoundations of social phenomena' (ibid., p. 83).[36] There are also many other theorists who take into account the interactive influences of the environment on individual behavior. For instance, as Levine, Sober and Wright point out, there are 'Theories of socialization which emphasize the inculcation of norms, habits and rituals' (ibid., p. 82). Geoff Hodgson (1986) and Anthony Giddens (1985) are also both sympathetically critical of methodological individualism. Each rejects the drastic reductionism of Elster and Roemer, as each sees merit in searching for the social determinants of individual behavior. They advocate, in different ways, that social analysis should involve a study of how the social structure affects individual behavior and *vice versa*. Robert Paul Wolff (1990) argues that methodological individualism is unable to explain collective action, and that Elster's attempt to explain consciousness and collective action through reference to Prisoner's Dilemma games and the free rider problem are doomed to fail. In contrast, Wolff takes a position akin to Elster's more recent one regarding the role social norms play in explanation, and argues that collective action and consciousness depend on the individuals being mutually aware of shared efforts and values. The important question for Wolff is how these shared social values arise and this, he argues, cannot be explained by reference solely to methodological individualism and the assumption of egoistic behavior.

The common motivation for the advocacy of methodological individualism, or microfoundations, in Marxism is, as has been argued, the desire to avoid the teleology and expressive causality of Hegel which has characterized much of the history of Marxism. Thus, Elster, and others call for an analysis beginning from the specification of individual agents and their dispositions, beliefs, etc. However, as has been pointed out above, the deployment of methodological individualism in formal Marxian analyses subverts the desired 'agency' of the individuals to a structural determination specific to their respective positions in the model. As a result, a tension still persists between the role of the agent and the role of the environment, or structure. That is why there is a call by some, i.e. Przeworski, etc., for an interactive microfoundations which has room for both individual agency and societal influences. There has been another tradition within Marxism, of course, which has similarly sought to understand the interactive nature of individual and structure, or part and whole. That is the tradition of, among others, Althusser and Balibar, Hindess and Hirst, Resnick and Wolff, and Laclau and Mouffe. They all, albeit in different ways, attempt to understand the social totality as a decentered, contingent, and nonteleological entity that is not governed by any pregiven essence or inherent rationality. The approach of these theorists will be developed in more detail in the next chapter, and subsequently the implications of this work for the way in which one can conceive the relationship between technical change and the rate of profit will be drawn out.

Conclusion

The debate over Marx's theory of the TRPF has now come full circle. Chapter 2 argued that the traditional debate over the TRPF was informed, shaped and structured according to the basic theoretical protocols of the ontological assumption of the Hegelian totality, as identified there. This chapter has reported on a remarkable shift in the terrain of the debate over the TRPF over the last 20 years or so. The Okishio theorem, and the issues over which debates and extensions of the theorem have been centered, have subtly, and sometimes forcefully, given rise to a new ontological structure through which the growth, development and crisis tendencies of capitalism are to be understood.

The Cartesian approach to totality, which assumes that parts are prior to wholes, stands in opposition to the Hegelian approach to totality, where wholes determine and prefigure parts. As Elster and other strict adherents to the Cartesian approach insist, societies do not exist, only individuals. By adopting a strict reductionist methodological program, as did those in the previous chapter, yet now inverting the direction of reduction, new issues of debate, research and even, one might say, a new problematic, have emerged through which the relationship between capitalist development and profit can be investigated. As has been argued in this chapter, this shift of terrain has given rise to a new Marxian paradigm and with it a new set of concepts and problems. The very meaning of concepts such as capital, accumulation, and the value rate of profit have now been transformed into new ones, tinged with Cartesian and Okishian meaning, of the rational capitalist, technical change and the Sraffian uniform rate of profit.

Where does the debate over the TRPF stand now as a result of this shift in terrain? Has the Okishio theorem sounded the death knell for the traditional debate over the TRPF? Perhaps so, but if it has, it is not because the Okishio theorem has 'disproved' the traditional story about the TRPF as outlined in Chapter 2. Rather, as has been argued in this chapter, the

Okishio theorem has served as a handmaiden to the broader paradigm shift taking place within Marxism, where some are casting off their Hegelian past for the hope of a bright Cartesian future. Thus, one can speak of the Okishio theorem as 'displacing' the traditional approach to the TRPF, and thereby rendering this erstwhile debate passé. It would, however, be a mistake to lay it to rest for good, as different theoretical approaches recur, oscillate and spring forth revitalized as new questions are raised and old, unresolved questions are revisited (witness the rebirth of Classical macroeconomics as 'new' Classical macroeconomics, and Keynesian economics as 'new' Keynesian macroeconomics).

Indeed, there are already signs of a change in approach with the rediscovery of social norms, institutions and structures. Those who have pushed the Cartesian approach to its frontier have now realized that not all aspects of social life can be reduced to individuals, understood as social atoms, but that norms and institutions exert their own independent causal effect on the constitution and trajectory of the social totality. However, the introduction of Cartesian and methodological individualist approaches within Marxian theory have served notice that theories which subvert the intentions and volitions of individuals to some grand, overarching teleological developmental process of structures, or of History, are viewed by most Marxists today as inadequate and onesided. Increasingly, there are calls for a more interactive social theory, where part and structure interpenetrate and codetermine each other. Such calls resonate the longstanding, but too often forgotten, commitment of Marxian theory to dialectics, however, now shorn of its association with cosmic theories of teleology. Indeed, this reinscribing of the dialectical and interactive methodological approach of Marxian theory had begun to be revitalized in the early 1960s with Althusser's deployment of the concepts of overdetermination and complex contradiction which prefigured just such a methodological position, one which would steer an uneasy path between the grand teleology of Hegel and its counterpoint of theoretical humanism.

The final chapter of this book will develop an approach to social totality which reduces neither whole to part nor part to whole. The decentered concept of totality developed there will be used to reconstruct the relationship between accumulation, technical change and the rate of profit and thereby shift the Marxian debate in a new direction once again.

CHAPTER 4

A Decentered Marxist Approach to Totality and the Contradictory Movement of the Rate of Profit

The goal of this final chapter is to outline an alternative approach to understanding the social totality, one that neither reduces the effectivity of the parts to the inner logic of an independently constituted whole, nor reduces the whole to an aggregation of preexisting parts. Instead, the alternative totality which will be put forth derives from the ontological premise that neither parts nor whole can exist independently from the other. Each part will be understood to exist only insofar as it is the effect of the interaction of all the other processes in the totality. Likewise, each part is understood to partially determine the existence of all the other parts in the totality. In other words, all the parts, and therefore the totality as well, mutually condition one another. Neither part nor totality can exist prior to the other. This concept of totality is what Louis Althusser referred to as a decentered totality in his influential essay 'Contradiction and Overdetermination' (1979, p. 102).

The decentered approach to totality has not yet played a role in either the traditional or Okishio debates over the TRPF. This is not a surprising result since these two variants of the broader debate over the TRPF are based on the Hegelian and Cartesian approaches to totality respectively. The adoption by Marxist theorists of a decentered totality will dramatically alter the terms and issues of concern from those in either the traditional or Okishio debates. Indeed, the very concepts of enterprise, economy and technical change will take on irreducibly different meanings and significance in the context of a decentered totality.

In particular, the concept of a decentered totality gives new meaning to the concepts of enterprise and economy. Instead of being conceived as a part of the totality (economy), as the enterprise was in both the traditional and Okishio approaches to totality, the enterprise will now be conceived as a totality itself, insofar as it exists as the effect of all of its conditions of existence. Further, the enterprise will not be reduced to an expression of capitalism's inner essence (accumulation) as in the traditional debate over the TRPF, or reduced to a simple profit maximizing machine, as in the Okishio debate. Rather, the enterprise will be understood to be a complexly overdetermined and contradictory totality. The enterprise is the site of a variety of class and nonclass processes, none of which constitute its essence. The rate of profit is equally overdetermined by these conditions of existence, and therefore there is no unidirectional, or teleological direction, whether up or down, inherent in its movement.

The concept of an economy as a homogeneous space on which the actions of enterprises are acted out cannot be sustained in the context of a decentered totality. In fact, the idea that there is a homogeneous totality called 'the economy', whether as a mode of production or an equilibrium system, is rejected in this approach. Enterprises are understood to be uniquely constituted with respect to their economic (class and nonclass aspects) and noneconomic conditions of existence. As a result, the 'social space' or economic environment in which they operate is a complexly constituted and contradictory one, which in no way can be reduced to its economic aspects.

This chapter represents only a first step in rethinking the relationship between technical change, the enterprise and the rate of profit. Once it is admitted that the enterprise is a complex entity, composed of class and nonclass aspects, then the analysis of its reproduction and change requires a detailed and constantly changing analysis as new conditions of existence are considered. There is no theoretical fixed point to which an analyst can comfortably return in order to guarantee knowledge. In the world of decentered totalities, a constant vigilance must be maintained as new theories and 'truths' are always just around the corner.

Althusser and the Concept of a Decentered Totality

The concept of a decentered totality can be traced to Althusser, and subsequently has been developed in different ways by, among others, Hindess and Hirst, Laclau and Mouffe, and Resnick and Wolff respectively.[1] The work of these theorists has provided the theoretical space to construct a nonreductionist approach to Marxian social theory, which allows for the reconstruction and shifting of the debate over the TRPF. In particular, Resnick and Wolff, building on the work of Althusser, have constructed a decentered Marxist approach to totality which is especially appropriate for understanding the relationship between technical change and the rate of profit. This approach to social causality and the decentered totality of Resnick and Wolff will be outlined below in order to flesh out in more detail the alternative relationship between the rate of profit and technical change which will be developed in the latter part of the chapter.

Before proceeding, however, it is important to sketch out briefly the development of the concept of a decentered totality as put forward by Althusser, in order to see what is at stake in this changed ontological ground (changed from the Hegelian and Cartesian approaches). In order to best understand the meaning of the decentered or, as Althusser called it, the Marxist totality, it is useful to distinguish it from the Hegelian totality. It was in Althusser's influential essays, 'Contradiction and Overdetermination' and 'Towards a Materialist Dialectic' where this distinction was best developed.[2]

What, then, are these differences between the Hegelian and Marxist totalities? For Althusser, the conceptual differences between the Marxist and the Hegelian totalities were dramatic. Indeed, he claimed that 'All these two "totalities" have in common is: (1) a word; (2) a certain vague conception of the unity of things; (3) some theoretical enemies' (1979, p. 203). The main theoretical enemy that they shared was theoretical humanism. The dominant variant of theoretical humanism to which Althusser directed his attention is a form of methodological individualism, as it derives its social explanations on the actions of preexisting subjects, as in the approach of the Cartesian totality detailed in Chapter 3. This shared enemy of the Hegelian and Marxist totalities reveals, simultaneously, the similarity between them. As Althusser argued, 'Marx was close to Hegel in his insistence on rejecting every philosophy of the Origin and of the Subject, whether rationalist, empiricist or transcendental' (1975, p. 178).

However, while Hegel rejected philosophies based on an Origin, he nonetheless maintained, according to Althusser, a concept of a telos guiding history:

> the Hegelian dialectic rejects every Origin, which is what is said at the beginning of the *Logic*, where Being is immediately identified with Nothingness, it projects this into the End of a Telos which in return creates, within its own process, its own Origin and its own Subject. (ibid., p. 180)

In contrast to the Hegelian totality, Althusser's Marxist totality was one which could not be reduced either to the effect of an Origin, or be guided by a teleological principle of development. That is, Althusser's Marxist totality neither reduces the parts to an expression of the whole, as does the Hegelian totality, nor the whole to the aggregation of its independently constituted parts, as does the Cartesian totality. Instead, the Marxist totality is to be thoroughly nonessentialist as the parts (contradictions for Althusser) mutually constitute one another.

In the chapter 'On the Materialist Dialectic' in *For Marx* (1979), Althusser constructs in detail his Marxist concept of totality by comparing the Marxist to the Hegelian notions of unity. He insists that for the Marxist totality

'There is no longer any original essence, only an ever-pre-giveness, however far knowledge delves into its past ... There is no longer any simple unity (in any form whatsoever), but instead, *the ever-pre-giveness of a structured complex unity*' (ibid., pp. 198–9). By the ever-pre-giveness of the unity Althusser means that there can be no beginning (essence), nor end (telos), to the historical development of the totality. That the Marxist totality is to be conceived as a 'structured, complex unity' implies further that there must be some unifying principle which sutures the totality into a unity (structured unity) yet does not in turn reduce this unity to an effect of a causal essence (complex unity). That is, the suture plays a binding role for the totality; it gives the totality a unity without reducing it to an expression of itself.

Althusser applies the notion of the Marxist totality directly to the analysis of society, or social formation. He maintains that the society's contradictions mutually and unevenly constitute one another. In particular, he discusses how the forces and the relations of production overdetermine each other and, in turn, overdetermine the superstructure.

> As an example, take the complex structured whole that is society. In it, the 'relations of production' are not the pure phenomena of the forces of production; they are also their condition of existence. The superstructure is not the pure phenomena of the structure, it is also its condition of existence. This follows from Marx's principle ... that production without society, that is, without social relations, exists nowhere; that we can go no deeper than the unity that is the unity of a whole in which, if the relations of production do have production itself as their condition of existence, production has as its condition of existence its form: the relations of production. (ibid., p. 205)

On the one hand, Althusser here is renouncing technological determinism (the relations of production are not the pure phenomena of the forces), and on the other hand economic determinism (the superstructure is not the pure phenomenon of the economic structure). Again, he stresses the mutual conditioning of all the contradictions of the totality. However, he maintains emphatically that this does not vitiate the importance of the concept of the structure in dominance. He insists that the structure in dominance is critical for the very concept of a whole to exist at all. He continues by imploring that this point not be misunderstood.

> Please do not misunderstand me: this mutual conditioning of the existence of the 'contradictions' does not nullify the structure in dominance that reigns over the contradictions and in them (in this case, [society] determination in the last instance by the economy). Despite its apparent circularity, this conditioning does not result in the destruction of the

structure of domination that constitutes the complexity of the whole, and its unity. Quite the contrary, even within the reality of the conditions of existence of each contradiction, it is the manifestation of the structure in dominance that unifies the whole. (ibid., pp. 205–6)

This certainly appears to be a paradoxical claim. On the one hand, it is claimed that the contradictions of society mutually constitute each other. Yet, at the same time, Althusser insists that a structure in dominance reigns over them and in them, determined in the last instance by the economy. Does this not imply a form of economic determinism has remained, even if ever so slightly, in Althusser's analysis? Certainly his insistence of the determination by the economy in the last instance, even if 'From the first moment to the last, the lonely hour of the "last instance" never comes' (1979, p. 113), has been the source of much criticism.[3]

Indeed, Althusser is often criticized, even by his most sympathetic interpreters, for retaining an economic determinism despite his concerted attempts to avoid any such determinism. This claim is made for instance by Hindess and Hirst, who attribute Althusser's inconsistency to the rationalist epistemology they read in him (Hindess and Hirst, 1977b). Similarly, Laclau and Mouffe argue that Althusser slips into the very rationalist epistemology from which he is otherwise at such pains to distance himself. They write that:

if society does have a last and essential determination ... the social is unified in the sutured space of a rationalist paradigm. Thus, we are confronted with exactly the same dualism that we found reproduced since the end of the nineteenth century in the field of Marxist discursiveness. (1985, p. 99)

Resnick and Wolff, who read Althusser as rejecting both empiricist and rationalist epistemologies, nevertheless still recognize a latent economic determinism. They write that:

However, freed of these epistemological aspects, a kind of economic determinist argument still survives, although just barely, in Althusser's formulation of Marxian theory. The clearest statement of this argument emerges in his conception of the overdetermined social totality as a structure of instances or aspects 'articulated in dominance,' namely, the last-instance dominance of the economic aspects over the noneconomic. How such a formulation could possibly be reconciled with an antiessentialist notion of Marxian theory remains an unanswered problem in Althusser's work. (1987, p. 93)

It appears that Althusser, despite his concerted attempts to the contrary, could not completely decenter his concept of the Marxist totality. The determination by the economy in the last instance remained for him an anchor without which the Marxist totality would drift away. It would remain for others (in particular, Hindess and Hirst, and Resnick and Wolff), to cast off completely from the treacherous shoals of economic determinism (even if only in the last instance). Despite his failure to rid Marxism completely of its economism, Althusser certainly took this project in a long, and progressive, direction.

The Decentered Totality of Resnick and Wolff

Stephen Resnick and Richard Wolff in their *Knowledge and Class* (1987) have gone furthest in applying the concept of a decentered totality to economic issues. They develop in this book a concept of the decentered totality and a nonessentialist approach to social causality, and then apply these ideas to traditional Marxist ideas of the working class, the fragmentation of the capitalist class, the theory of the enterprise and the theory of the state. As these concepts structure the discussion below about the rate of profit, it is important to develop them in some detail here. This will also bring out the differences of this approach from the Hegelian and Cartesian approaches to totality as developed in Chapters 2 and 3.

Resnick and Wolff begin by defining society as the totality of all the processes which comprise it. A process for them is the basic element of analysis, the fundamental discursive primitive, which are grouped for convenience into economic, political, cultural and natural categories. Processes, however, can never exist alone. They always occur in particular configurations with other processes. Resnick and Wolff call such configured sets of processes relationships. Relationships, and therefore processes, always occur together in particular conceptual locations called sites. Examples of sites include the individual, the family, a university, a church, the US Congress, a capitalist enterprise, a society, etc. A site is literally a conceptually defined place where groups of relationships occur and whose effects constitute the site.

Resnick and Wolff retain Althusser's basic causal concepts of overdetermination and contradiction. For them no process, and therefore no relationship, exists prior to or independently from any other process or relationship. Each process exists, literally, as the site of effects emanating from all the other processes in society. Each process also contributes in part to the existence of all the other processes in society. This reciprocal multisided causality, or mutual constitution, is what Resnick and Wolff, following Althusser, refer to as overdetermination. As each process is uniquely constituted by its particular overdetermination, each process moves in a complex and contradictory manner. That is to say, as one process changes so too do all the others, and therefore any one process is in a constant, non-teleological flux, overdetermined time and again by the continual, contradictory movement of its conditions of existence (processes).

As relationships are particular collections of processes, and sites are locations where relationships and processes occur, they, too, are overdetermined and contradictory. This implies that for a given society (i.e. a particular collection of sites delimited by a national boundary), its history will be characterized by an uneven development. A society's development is not conceived in a teleological manner, as it was in the context of the Hegelian totality. Nor is society conceived as the equilibrium configuration which emerges from the interaction of preexisting parts, as in the Cartesian approach. Society's law of development is, instead, the law of uneven development. It is the continual constitution and reconstitution of uniquely overdetermined sites.[4]

Resnick and Wolff insist that a Marxist social totality is to be conceived as 'a relation of overdetermined part to overdetermined whole' (1987, p. 9). The strict distinction between part and whole, however, becomes blurred in their overdetermined discourse. Each process of society exists only insofar as it is the site of effects from all the other processes in society. At the same time, each process is a necessary constituent aspect of all the other processes in society. Thus, a process is both determining, and determined by, the other processes. A process is both a part and a whole. A process reflects in itself the totality of society's contradictions, and therefore in that sense is itself a totality. Yet each process is constituted differently from all the other processes and, therefore, also can be conceived as a part.

The distinction between part and whole is one which is only strictly appropriate in the Cartesian and Hegelian reductionist approaches to social totality. There, an unambiguous dichotomy is made between part and whole, as one is conceived to be the causal essence of the other. However, in a decentered totality, neither part nor whole exists independently from the other. As Resnick and Wolff insist, each is overdetermined by the other. This blurring of the distinction between part and whole is not unlike what an overdetermined epistemology does to the ontological gap between the thought process and material reality; it denies that such a gap exists. Just as the approach of an overdetermined epistemology rejects the ontological distinction between theory and material reality, so too does the approach of a decentered totality and an overdetermined causality deny the strict distinction between part and whole. Indeed, one is left with the vexing question of whether, in the process of decentering the Marxist totality, the Marxist totality disappears altogether.

Gregory Elliot echoes this same concern in his comment on Althusser where he asks:

What therefore remains of the classical Marxist thesis of ultimate economic determination – the thesis with which Marx demarcated his theory of history from idealist philosophies? And if the regions of the decentered, non-homogeneous social totality are composed of distinct practices, irreducible – spatially and temporally – to one another, is this totality a bona fide totality or a congeries of discrete interacting elements? Has pluralism, so to speak, been substituted for historical materialism? Althusser insisted that his concept of the social whole was Marxist and was a totality – albeit one that is simultaneously complex and unified, decentered and determined, heterogeneous and hierarchical. (Elliot, 1987, p. 155)

If the decentered, Marxist totality is indeed composed of a complex set of different and heterogeneous processes, none of which can be reduced to the other, what gives each totality its distinct shape, and in particular what marks a specific totality as Marxist and thereby avoids the pluralism to which Elliott refers? Resnick and Wolff provide an answer with their insistence on the class process (defined as the performance, appropriation, and distribution of surplus labor) as the specific *entry-point* of Marxist theory. Resnick and Wolff define the concept of entry-point as 'that particular concept a theory uses to enter into its formulation, its particular construction of entities and relations that comprise the social totality' (1987, p. 25). The class process as entry-point does not act as a causal essence for Resnick and Wolff, but instead serves the role of a philosophical primitive. It is a concept which gives a particular discourse its shape and focus, the basic organizing concept in and through which the Marxist totality is constructed. Thus, Resnick and Wolff share with Althusser a commitment to a nonessentialist, decentered and Marxist social totality. However, they differ from Althusser by rejecting any notion of last instance determination by the economy, structure in dominance, or the differentiation between principal and secondary contradictions. The concept of entry-point allows Resnick and Wolff to avoid the last instance determinism of Althusser and at the same time avoid the radical pluralism or relativism that so often is attributed to those rejecting the metaphysical foundationalism of traditional approaches to social theory.

The Decentered Totality: Enterprise and Economy

Chapter 2 argued that the enterprise was conceived to be a part, 'capital', which expressed the economy's (understood as a pregiven and structured totality) inner essence, accumulation. In Chapter 3, the enterprise was conceived to be a part; however, now, understood to be a rational capitalist who existed prior to and independently of the totality. The totality, in fact, was conceived to be nothing more than the equilibrium configuration which emerged from the interaction of the preconstituted parts. However, as argued above, the causal distinction between part and whole is inappropriate in the context of a decentered totality. Indeed, all sites can now be conceived as totalities as each site exists as the effect of all the processes which constitute it. In particular, the enterprise *qua* site is no longer to be conceived as a part, but now rather as a totality, and in so doing the meaning and significance of the concepts of enterprise and economy change dramatically from those used in the traditional debate over the TRPF, as well as those used in the Okishio debate.

A capitalist enterprise is a site, and as such is also a decentered totality.[5] An industrial capitalist enterprise, hereafter simply capitalist enterprise, is the site of what Resnick and Wolff call the capitalist fundamental and subsumed class processes as well as the site of other political, cultural, natural and economic processes (see Resnick and Wolff, 1987, pp. 166–70). The capitalist fundamental class process can be defined as the production and appropriation of surplus value, while the capitalist subsumed class process refers to the first distribution of the already appropriated surplus value. The fundamental and subsumed class processes can be represented in the following surplus value/subsumed class payment expenditure equation:

$$S = \sum_{i=1}^{N} SC_i$$

where S represents surplus value, and SC_i represents the ith subsumed class payment of the 'n' distributions of surplus value which the capitalist enterprise makes. In order for the capitalist enterprise to reproduce itself, it must distribute its surplus value in such a way as to satisfy a number of various conditions of existence. For example, the capitalist enterprise may have to make payments to managers in charge of accumulation, supervision, finances, advertising, political lobbying, etc. Further, the capitalist enterprise may also have to make subsumed class payments to individuals outside its legal boundaries such as rental payments to landlords, interest payments to bond-holders, taxes to various governmental institutions, etc. Each payment is made in order to procure a specific condition of existence of the capitalist enterprise, and therefore the continued production of surplus value. Again, to emphasize, the capitalist enterprise is literally the site of all these effects, and in this sense the enterprise is understood as a decentered totality.

The essence of the capitalist enterprise cannot be reduced to any specific subsumed class payment. In particular, accumulation is not the essence of the capitalist enterprise, to which all the other subsumed class payments are so many phenomenal appearances.[6] Each subsumed class payment contributes a particular effect to the existence of the capitalist enterprise, and a change in any one will change the trajectory of the capitalist enterprise. The decision-making process within the capitalist enterprise with respect to the exact configuration of subsumed class distributions is an overdetermined process affected by managers, productive workers, the board of directors, etc. within the capitalist enterprise, and by others outside it, such as legislators, bank presidents, anti-nuke activists, etc. As a result, the particular subsumed class distributions of a capitalist enterprise will constantly change over time as the influence and interests of these individuals change.

Each capitalist enterprise is uniquely constituted with respect to both its internal and external conditions of existence. That is, each capitalist enterprise has a unique management structure, forms of control, labor process, personalities of management and workers, history of labor relations and so on. Likewise, each capitalist enterprise faces a distinct external environment. Each capitalist enterprise will have different relations with financial and government institutions, each will face different market conditions, each will enjoy different degrees of product recognition, different firms will have differential relationships with competitors within and without the same industry, each will be owned by different sets of stockholders, etc. In other words, in this approach there is no meaning to the concept of a 'representative' capitalist enterprise that exists in a homogeneous space called the 'economy'. Rather, each capitalist enterprise is the unique site of the overdetermination of its particular conditions of existence.

The fact that each capitalist enterprise is unique implies that the notion of an economy as a homogeneous space in which all face the same conditions of existence (at least within an industry) is no longer tenable. In contrast, in Chapter 2 the economy was conceived as a mode of production which had definite economy-wide effects on all capitalist enterprises, i.e. a capitalist enterprise's purpose was to act as a site of accumulation. Chapter 3 argued that the economy was a homogeneous competitive space which generated, in combination with the rational profit-maximizing actions of individual capitalists, an economy-wide, equal (or uniform) rate of profit which all enterprises earned in equilibrium.

However, if all capitalist enterprises are uniquely constituted, facing differential internal and external conditions of existence, the trajectory of the enterprises over time will be characterized by uneven development. Each capitalist enterprise is uniquely affected by its internal class and nonclass structure, as well as the actions of other capitalist enterprises and non-industrial capitalist enterprises. Furthermore, it is not only the so-called 'economic' institutions such as other enterprises, financial institutions, etc. that affect a particular capitalist enterprise's behavior. A capitalist enterprise's behavior is also in part determined by such 'noneconomic' entities as the various governing bodies of the state, as well as various educational, religious and sporting institutions, and so on. All these economic and noneconomic conditions of existence have determinate and unique effects on any particular capitalist enterprise. As such, each and every capitalist enterprise develops in a singular manner. Again, to stress, there is no typical or 'representative' capitalist enterprise, as was the case in the traditional debate over the TRPF where a 'capital's' role was to accumulate, or in the Okishio debate where all capitalists shared the same goal of profit and norm of maximization.

The idea that there is an economy in which the capitalist enterprise exists and which has determinate effects on the capitalist enterprise independent from other 'non-economic' aspects of society is now certainly a problematic one. Not only is the economy not a homogeneous space, the very concept of an economy as such, existing somehow independently from the rest of society, with its own 'economic' logic, cannot be sustained in the context of the decentered totality as outlined in this chapter. As a result, the terrain of debate of either the traditional approach to the TRPF or the Okishio theorem is no longer applicable. In other words, if one accepts the approach of a decentered totality in the tradition of Althusser and Resnick and Wolff, then the issues of debate in Chapters 2 and 3 are at a minimum now nonissues, or more strongly, literally nonsensical ones.

In particular, the focus of analysis would no longer be on tracing out the effects of a discovered essence such as accumulation or profit maximization on the homogeneous terrain of a mode of production or competitive economy. Rather, the focus of analysis would be on developing a framework through which to understand the potential contradictory results of the overdetermined action of a uniquely constituted capitalist enterprise, or even sets of capitalist enterprises. The focus would also be on understanding the overdetermined strategies of a given capitalist enterprise, and then analyzing the potential contradictory effects that such a strategy would have on the rate of profit.

The rate of profit, understood in this decentered context, would not be interpreted as reflecting the essential health or rationality of a capitalist enterprise, but rather the profit rate would simply be one measure of the nature of class relations in the capitalist enterprise, i.e. a measure of the amount of productive capital and labor needed to produce a certain amount of surplus value. No necessary implication for the nature of the class struggle, the health of the capitalist enterprise or whatever can be deduced from this measure of class relations. To make such a statement, the rate of profit must be considered in conjunction with all its other class and nonclass conditions of existence at a specific conjunctural moment, as is true with all other summary statistics like the unemployment rate, the gross national product or the rate of exploitation.

Furthermore, the claim that a capitalist enterprise's strategic decision-making is overdetermined implies that movements in the rate of profit are similarly overdetermined. That is, the precise pattern of distribution of subsumed class payments of a capitalist enterprise at any moment in time will affect the movement in the rate of profit. At the same time, movements in the rate of profit will affect the way in which subsumed class payments are distributed by the capitalist enterprise. This overdetermined effect can be seen by reconsidering the surplus value/subsumed class distribution equation. Divide each side of this equation by (C + V) to get the following expression for the rate of profit:

$$S/(C+V) = \sum_{i=1}^{N} SC_i / (C+V)$$

This equation can be simplified as:

$$e/(k+1) = \sum_{i=1}^{N} SC_i / (C+V)$$

Here, $e = S/V$, is the rate of exploitation, and $k = C/V$, is the organic composition of capital. On the right hand side of this equation are the various subsumed class payments which in part overdetermine both the rate of exploitation and the organic composition of capital. As the precise configuration of these subsumed class payments changes, so too will e and k, and hence the rate of profit. One example of the importance of subsumed class payments other than accumulation on the rate of profit would be the effect of decreased distributions to supervision managers in charge of maintaining the intensity of the productive laborers. As was pointed out in Chapter 2, the traditional debate over the TRPF focused exclusively on the effect of only one of these subsumed class payments, accumulation, on the organic composition of capital and the rate of exploitation, and hence on the rate of profit, to the exclusion of the effect of all the other subsumed class payments. In Chapter 3 it was the focus on technical change, different, yet related to the traditional Marxian concept of the accumulation of capital that was the focus of debate. The decentered concept of totality put forward in this chapter, along with the concept of class process as entry-point, makes it possible to reconstruct the traditional and Okishio debates over the rate of profit, and in so doing open up new terrain and issues for debate. The next section of this chapter begins this reconstruction.

The Contradictory Effect of Accumulation on the Rate of Profit

Given its importance in the literature over the TRPF, the two examples presented here will explore the contradictory effects of accumulation on the rate of profit. The first example will analyze the effect on the rate of profit of a redistribution of surplus value from supervision to accumulation in a static and partial setting, where unit values are held constant. The second example will incorporate the dynamic effect of the cheapening of constant and variable capital as a result of productivity gains due to the accumulation of capital.

Example 1: Redistribution of Surplus Value in a Static Setting

Assume that an industrial capitalist enterprise decides to increase subsumed class payments to those managers in charge of accumulation. Perhaps the enterprise undertakes such a strategy because it hopes to raise its rate of profit through increased exploitation of productive laborers. The exact motive is unimportant for the present analysis.

The decision of the capitalist enterprise to accumulate will engender a series of potentially contradictory effects which may in fact undermine or alter the original intent of the increased accumulation, in this case an increase in the rate of profit. Indeed, it is entirely possible that any attempt by the enterprise to raise the rate of profit through increased subsumed class payments to accumulation may set in motion forces which actually lower the rate of profit.

In order to see this contradictory process clearly, assume for simplicity that the capitalist enterprise makes only two subsumed class payments: a share of surplus value goes to managers to secure the economic process of accumulation and another share of surplus value goes to secure the political process of the supervision of the production process. Assume, also purely for simplicity, that unit exchange values are constant and that the real wage is constant and equal for all productive laborers.

Now, by undertaking a strategic decision to increase subsumed class payments to managers in charge of accumulation, the capitalist enterprise hopes that more surplus value will be produced, and/or realized, in future periods and as a result its rate of profit will increase. A change in the amount of surplus value produced may occur in two ways. On the one hand, surplus value production may rise because more productive labor is employed, thereby producing more total value and total surplus value (assuming no change in the rate of exploitation). On the other hand, if the intensity of labor is increased (due to increased supervision of productive labor), then relative surplus value will be produced as productive laborers can reproduce their living standard in a shorter part of the working day. Also, if accumulation is such that productive laborers can work more efficiently (more use values produced per hour worked), then the innovating enterprise will realize 'super profits' and its 'realized rate of exploitation' will rise.[7]

Assume, further, that in order to increase subsumed class payments to accumulation, there must be at the same time a reduction in surplus value distributions to supervisory managers by an equivalent amount. Assume that the decreased distribution of surplus value results in supervisors being laid off. This, in turn, will decrease the rate of exploitation as productive laborers will now work less intensely (assuming a positive correlation between the amount of supervision and the intensity of labor), and therefore not produce as much surplus value as previously. Thus there is, even in this simple example, the possibility of contradictory effects on the enterprise's rate of profit as accumulation increases. These contradictory effects are the result of the mutual interaction, or overdetermination, of the specific conditions of existence of the capitalist enterprise. In this example, only the subsumed class process of accumulation and the subsumed class process of supervision combine to overdetermine the enterprise's rate of profit. In a more elaborate example, one would have to specify the potential interactions and reactions of all the theorized conditions of existence as they respond to the initial change in accumulation.

The contradictory effect of accumulation on the rate of profit in the above example can be expressed formally as follows. Let the already appropriated surplus value, S, be exhaustively distributed to accumulation managers, SC_a, and supervisors, SC_s. Thus, the surplus value distribution equation can be written as

$$S = SC_a + SC_s$$

Define the rate of profit for the capitalist enterprise as

$$r = S/(C + V)$$
$$= e/(k + 1)$$

Where:

$e = S/V$ and $k = C/V$.

The rate of exploitation, e, is a positive function of both SC_a (due to realization of super profits) and SC_s (due to the assumption that supervision increases the intensity of productive labor). The rate of exploitation, then, can be expressed as

$$e = e(SC_a, SC_s) \text{ where } e_1 > 0 \text{ and } e_2 > 0.$$

By definition, the accumulation of capital is equal to the increase in productive capital and productive labor. The organic composition of capital, k, changes depending on the labor or capital bias of the accumulation process. Thus the organic composition of capital can be written as a function of the subsumed class payment to accumulation.

$k = k(SC_a)$ where $SC_a = \Delta C + \Delta V$.

As accumulation proceeds, $k' \gtreqless 0$ (where $k = dk/dSC_a$), depending on whether the organic composition of capital is rising (accumulation is biased towards capital), staying the same (accumulation is neutral) or falling (accumulation is biased towards labor).[8]

The rate of profit can now be expressed explicitly as a function of SC_a and SC_s as follows:

$$r = e(SC_a, SC_s)/(k(SC_a) + 1)$$

By partially differentiating this equation with respect to SC_a, the following result can be obtained.

$$\partial r / \partial SC_a = \frac{(e_1 + e_2(dSC_s / dSC_a))(k+1) - ek'}{(g+1)^2}$$

The above equation can be simplified as follows:[9]

$$\partial r / \partial SC_a = \frac{(e_1 - e_2)(k+1) - ek'}{(g+1)^2}$$

As the denominator of this equation, $(k+1)^2$, is always positive, the sign of the partial derivative, $\partial r/\partial SC_a$, depends only on the sign of the numerator. Thus, the movement of the rate of profit in response to an increase in the subsumed class payment to accumulation depends on the relative sizes of the following three factors:

1. *The accumulation effect* (e_1): the increase in the rate of exploitation due to the increased efficiency of the productive laborers and the subsequent realization of super profits.
2. *The supervision effect* (e_2): the decrease in the rate of exploitation due to the decreased efficiency of the productive laborers as supervisory labor is reduced.
3. *The change in the organic composition of capital* (k'): the organic composition of capital may rise, fall or stay the same depending on the capital, labor, or lack of, bias of the technical change.

The potential changes of the rate of profit can be analyzed in three different cases, depending on whether the organic composition of capital rises, falls or remains the same.

Case I: $k' > 0$

This is the usual assumption made in the literature, i.e. the organic composition of capital rises as accumulation proceeds. Mathematically, the assumption of $k' > 0$, implies that the second term in the numerator is always negative. Therefore, the rate of profit will rise, stay the same or fall, according to the following conditions:

(a) $\partial r / \partial SC_a < 0$, if either (i) $e_2 > e_1$. That is, the supervision effect is greater than the accumulation effect, and therefore the numerator is negative, or (ii) $e_1 > e_2$ (the accumulation effect is greater than the supervision effect), and $k'/(k + 1) > (e_1 - e_2)/e$, i.e. the rate of growth of the organic composition of capital is greater than the net rate of growth of the rate of exploitation. Thus, the rate of profit will fall if either (i) the decreased amount of surplus value production, due to the negative supervision effect, is greater than the increased surplus value production due to the positive accumulation effect, or (ii) the accumulation effect is greater than the supervision effect, and also the rate of growth of net surplus value production is less than the rate of growth of the organic composition of capital.

(b) $\partial r / \partial SC_a > 0$, if $e_1 > e_2$ and $(e_1 - e_2)/e > k'/(k + 1)$. That is, the rate of profit will not decrease if the positive accumulation effect is greater than the negative supervision effect, and the net rate of growth of the rate of exploitation is greater than or equal to the rate of growth of the organic composition of capital.

Case II: $k' < 0$

This is the case of a technical change which exhibits a capital-saving bias. Technical change of this sort implies that the productive labor input becomes more prevalent in the production process. In this case, the rate of profit will change according to the following conditions:

(a) $\partial r / \partial SC_a < 0$, if $e_2 > e_1$ and $(e_1 - e_2)/e > k'/(k + 1)$. That is, the rate of profit will fall as the organic composition of capital increases, if the negative supervision effect is greater than the positive accumulation effect, and simultaneously the net increase in the rate of exploitation is greater than the rate of decrease (as $k' < 0$) in the organic composition capital.

(b) $\partial r / \partial SC_a > 0$, if either (i) $e_1 > e_2$, or (ii) $e_2 > e_1$ and $k'/(k +1) > (e_1 - e_2)/e$. In this case, the rate of profit will rise as accumulation proceeds if either (i) the accumulation effect is at least as great as the supervision effect, or (ii) the supervision effect is greater than the accumulation effect and the rate of decrease in the organic composition of capital is greater than the net rate of growth of the rate of exploitation.

Case III: $k' = 0$

This is the case of 'neutral' technical change. That is, the percentage increase in constant capital is exactly equal to the percentage increase in variable capital as accumulation proceeds. The rate of profit will change according to the following straightforward condition: $\partial r/\partial SC_a > 0$ as $e_1 > e_2$. In this case, the movement of the rate of profit is only affected by the net change in the rate of exploitation depending on the relative movements of the accumulation and supervision effects.

Example 2: Redistribution of Surplus Value in a Dynamic Setting

The previous example considered the contradictory effect on the rate of profit of an enterprise when there is a redistribution of surplus value from supervision to accumulation. It was also assumed there that the per unit exchange values of constant and variable capital remained constant. Thus, the above example assumed a partial (in the sense of no interactive effects from other enterprises) and static (in the sense of no adjustments of unit values over time) setting. This allowed the highlighting of the contradictory effect of accumulation on the rate of profit. In a dynamic setting, however, the increase in productivity brought about by the increase in accumulation will tend to lower the unit values of capital and wage goods. This cheapening of constant and variable capital adds a different dimension to the overall contradictory effect on the rate of profit.

As was described in detail in Chapter 2, the cheapening of constant capital, and to a lesser extent the cheapening of variable capital, was one of the most debated 'counteracting causes' of the TRPF. It should be remembered that Sweezy, Robinson and others felt that any increase in the technical composition of capital would also lead to a rise in productivity and a fall in the unit value of the capital goods and the wage goods, and thereby lower the total value of constant and variable capital. Thus, there could be no assurance that the organic composition of capital would rise as a result of the accumulation of capital, even if the technical composition of capital were to rise. And, as a result, there could be no law of the tendency for the rate of profit to fall, understood as a *necessary* result of capital accumulation.

The position of Sweezy, Robinson and others makes sense in a partial and static setting where one interprets Marx's law of the TRPF as a necessary prediction following from capital accumulation. However, as Fine and Harris (1979) and, more recently, Fine (1990) and Saad-Filho (1993) argue, Marx made a distinction between his concept of the organic composition of capital and the value composition of capital. The organic composition of capital applied in a static and partial setting where the unit values of constant and variable capital were assumed to be constant as the technical composition of capital increased. The organic composition thus 'reflected' the changes in the technical composition of capital. In a dynamic, economy-wide setting, the productivity gains associated with a rising technical composition of capital would lower the unit values of both wage goods and capital goods and the resulting composition of capital, the value composition, would not directly reflect the increased technical composition of capital, and the value composition of capital can change in the opposite direction from the technical composition.

As shown in Chapter 2, the composition of capital can be written as

$$k = C/V$$
$$= (m/n)T$$

where m is the unit value of the capital good, n is the unit value of the wage good and T is the technical composition of capital.[10] It will be assumed here, as is commonly done in the literature, that as capital accumulation proceeds, the technical composition of capital, T, increases, and the unit values, m and n, decrease, although not necessarily at the same rate. If this is the case, the overall effect on the organic composition of capital will depend on the relative sizes of these rates of change.[11] The change in the organic composition of capital will depend on the value of the following equation

$$k = m - n + T$$

where k, m, n, and T are time rates of change as defined on page 43 in Chapter 2. The conditions under which the organic composition of capital will increase given the decrease in unit values were investigated in Chapter 2 and will not be repeated here.

Now consider an enterprise which redistributes its surplus value from distributions to supervision to distributions for accumulation, as in the above example. Assume that this increase in the accumulation of capital increases the technical composition of capital, raising productivity of the innovating enterprise. Given the increase in productivity, this innovation will be copied by other enterprises, and once this innovation is adopted by all relevant enterprises, new unit values for the wage goods and the capital goods will emerge.[12] The new rate of profit which will emerge in this case depends in part on the change in the technical composition of capital (the increase in the technical composition), in part on the decrease in surplus value produced due to the reduction in supervision (the supervision effect) and, finally, in part on the cheapening of constant and variable capital (the cheapening effect).

The mathematics for determining the overall effect on the rate of profit would be very complicated in this case and are not necessary for the point being made here: once the distribution of surplus value is considered, along with the cheapening of variable and constant capital, the overall effect on the rate of profit is contradictory. In the end, it depends on the relative sizes of the different effects under consideration.

These examples have demonstrated the complex and contradictory effects that the decision to increase subsumed class payments to accumulation managers, while simultaneously decreasing such payments to supervision managers, *might* have on the rate of profit. One must emphasize the word might, because conceiving of the capitalist enterprise as a decentered totality, as has been shown in this chapter, necessarily implies that there is no certainty accompanying any given initial change. The result of a particular capitalist enterprise's decision to accumulate will depend on the precise conjuncture of all its conditions of existence. Furthermore, the very action of accumulation will set in motion other reactions which may reinforce or work against the initial desired goal of raising the rate of profit. These rather simple examples have only considered the analysis of the contradictory relationship of these two conditions of existence on the rate of profit. A more concrete analysis, i.e. one which begins to incorporate more conditions of existence, both subsumed class payments and nonclass conditions of existence, would increasingly add complexity to the analysis. However, no matter how many conditions of existence are explicitly considered, it will never be possible to claim that the capitalist enterprise's essence has finally been discovered. An analysis of a decentered capitalist enterprise, and its conditions of existence, is never complete. It is always the case that its conditions of existence, complexly overdetermine each other, in a neverending contradictory process of uneven development.

Conclusion

Contrary to the essentialist straightjackets the Hegelian and Cartesian totalities impose, there is an alternative, nonreductionist way to conceive of a social totality. This approach to social totality differs from the Hegelian totality as it does not reduce the parts to an expression of a preexisting whole. It also differs from the Cartesian totality in that it does not derive the whole from a set of independently constituted parts. Rather, whole and part are conceived to mutually determine one another.

The decentered approach to totality has not been present in the debate over the TRPF or the Okishio theorem. Yet this approach to totality can play an important role in the debate. In particular, the decentered approach to totality can help alleviate a strangely paradoxical fate that has befallen the debate over the TRPF, whether in its traditional or Okishio version. On the one hand, the debate over the TRPF has been one of the most important and fiercely contested debates in Marxist economics. On the other hand, it is not difficult to see that this same debate has fallen into a period of stagnation and theoretical ennui. How is this possible when the debate concerns such important theoretical issues as the relationship between the rate of profit and a capitalist enterprise's competitive behavior? Or similarly, how could this debate have fallen into a period of stagnation when its participants have been concerned with such fundamental political questions as the reform versus revolution of capitalism? The answer lies in part in what the Hegelian and Cartesian totalities share in common, namely, their common commitment to a *reductionist* approach to social theory and causality.

This claim can be illustrated with two examples, one theoretical and the other political. Chapters 2 and 3 were concerned to demonstrate the important differences of how the capitalist enterprise was conceived in the traditional and Okishio debates respectively. It was shown how in the traditional debate the capitalist enterprise was assumed to be the site of accumulation, a role given to it by the inner essence of capitalism. In contrast, the Okishio debate understood the capitalist enterprise to be a site of profit maximization, a role which reflected the pregiven rationality of the capitalist enterprise. Chapters 2 and 3 thus stressed the differences among and between these two conceptualizations of the capitalist enterprise in order to show how they helped frame their respective debates differently. It is their *similarity*, however, that is important for understanding why the debate over the TRPF has become bogged down in recent years.

Each approach to the capitalist enterprise, whether as accumulator or profit maximizer, reduces the capitalist enterprise to a single goal whose realization is the essence of capitalist development. That is, each approach maintains a teleological understanding about capitalist behavior. The debate over the theory of the TRPF is then reduced to a debate over the logical consequences of the pregiven behavior of the capitalist enterprise. This debate has been, and continues to be, concerned with a wide variety of issues, as has been shown above, yet there remains a constant thread which indelibly weaves its imprint into both the traditional and Okishio debates, and that is its theory of the capitalist enterprise. It is assumed that the nature of the capitalist enterprise is a given, and it is only the economic environment which changes in the various analyses, and that environment never reacts back on the nature of the capitalist enterprise. In effect, this onesided approach closes down an important area of potential Marxist research concerning the dialectical or overdetermined interaction of the capitalist enterprise with its environment or conditions of existence.

It is possible to speculate briefly (and only briefly in this conclusion) on how the debate over the TRPF would be changed if the decentered approach to totality were applied to the relationship between the capitalist enterprise and the rate of profit. The capitalist enterprise in the context of a decentered totality would be conceived as a complex organization. That is, the capitalist enterprise would not be reduced to the expression of a single goal, but rather it would be understood as the site of the mutual interaction of class and nonclass processes. No process, whether class or nonclass, would act as the causal essence of the enterprise. All processes would exert their particular effectivity on the trajectory of the enterprise, and in particular all processes, not simply technical change, would effect the movement in the rate of profit. Thus the movement of the enterprise, as well as the rate of profit, would always be a complexly contradictory one. One effect of this way of conceiving the capitalist enterprise would be an opening up of the debate over the TRPF. No longer would the debate be solely concerned with the effect of technical change or accumulation on the rate of profit. Now, the focus of debate might be on how the capitalist enterprise reproduces itself over time and the effect of this reproduction on the rate of profit. The debate might concern itself, for example, with the political, cultural, financial, advertising and technical conditions for the successful reproduction of the capitalist enterprise. An important issue of debate might now be how the successful, or unsuccessful, reproduction of the capitalist enterprise changes the class structure of the capitalist enterprise, and how this is reflected in the rate of profit.

A related issue is how movements in the rate of profit are to be interpreted. In the traditional debate over the TRPF, the rate of profit was an index of the pace of accumulation, and *ipso facto* an index of the overall 'health' of capitalism. For the Okishio debate, the rate of profit was an index of the success of a 'rational' firm. Each profit rate reflected directly the inner essence of the Hegelian and Cartesian approaches respectively. However, in the context of a decentered totality, the capitalist enterprise has no such inner essence to be reflected. As a consequence, the rate of profit cannot act as an unambiguous index of the 'healthiness' or 'rationality' of the capitalist enterprise. Rather, the rate of profit is one index of the class structure of the capitalist enterprise. However, movements in the rate of profit cannot be unambiguously interpreted with respect to the reproduction or transition of the class structure of the capitalist enterprise. In order for such an analysis to occur, the rate of profit must be seen in its conjunctural specificity.[13]

Besides these more theoretical issues, the reductionism of the Hegelian and Cartesian approaches has had important and detrimental *political* consequences for the debate over the TRPF in particular, and Marxist crisis theory in general. The problem lies in the fact that the Hegelian and Cartesian totalities conceive of the economy as a unified or integrated whole. The economy, *qua* whole, is understood to be a site which develops uniformly over time. For example, capitalism (as a whole) may be reproduced over time, or alternatively capitalism (as a whole) may self-destruct and communism (as a whole) may emerge. Capitalist development may be reduced either to the driving force of accumulation or to the rationality of the individual capitalist. In either case, such causal essences are understood to have economy-wide effects. Thus, capitalism as a whole is either healthy or in crisis. Political analyses and strategies become, then, all-encompassing and totalizing recipes for change.

This way of conceiving of the economy is manifested politically in the debate over the TRPF in the issue of reform versus revolution. At issue is whether capitalism as a whole is capable of reform, or whether capitalism, again as a whole, must undergo a revolutionary transformation in order for its current oppressions to cease. As the rate of profit is directly linked to the overall health of the economy, its movement plays a crucial role in this debate. If the rate of profit falls as capitalism develops then, it is often argued, a revolution against capitalism will necessarily occur. However, if the rate of profit does not necessarily fall, then capitalism is capable of reform, and as some argue, the objective basis for the overthrow of capitalism is no longer tenable. As a result, the debate over the TRPF is often divided into the opposing camps of those (revolutionaries) who feel that the rate of profit must fall with capitalist development and those (reformists) who feel that there is no such necessity.

The political dichotomy of reform versus revolution, and the importance of the movement of the rate of profit, has its basis in the fundamental similarity between the Hegelian and Cartesian totalities. Each approach gives rise to a notion of the economy as a unified whole governed by either the essence of accumulation or capitalist rationality (profit maximization). The success of each economy is manifested in the movement of the rate of profit as the rate of profit is directly understood to reflect the health of the economy. If the rate of profit falls, capitalism is in crisis. If, however, the rate of profit rises, then capitalism is understood to be healthy. Thus, if the rate of profit falls, capitalism will undergo a revolutionary transformation. If not, then capitalism can reproduce and reform itself.

The concern in this book has not been to group people as to whether they feel that the rate of profit falls or not with capitalist development, but rather to group people as to how they conceive the nature of the social totality. As is now possible to see, this concern is partly due to political considerations. The decentered approach to totality rejects the notion of a social totality conceived as a unified whole. Instead, the decentered totality understands a society to be a contradictory amalgam of economic and noneconomic conditions of existence which are always in flux, but at the same time are not driven by any predetermined essence or telos. In other words, society always exists as a contradictory combination of changing and reproducing conditions of existence. As such society, on the one hand, is always undergoing a revolutionary transformation as all of its conditions of existence are constantly changing. Yet, on the other hand, there is no one condition of existence which can magically transform the fundamental nature of society, and therefore society is only ever capable of being reformed, or partially transformed.

This paradoxical situation of simultaneous revolution and reform reveals the limitations of these political categories in the context of the decentered totality. It is no longer possible to maintain such a strict bifurcation with respect to political strategy. Rather, political strategies and analyses must always focus on the conjunctural effects of changing specific conditions of existence of capitalism. As with the theoretical opening that the decentered totality brings to the debate over the TRPF, there is also a political opening up. Instead of a reliance on either the political copestone of a revolutionary transformation, or its opposite of an 'improved' capitalism, Marxist theorists interested in changing class structures will now be forced to analyze the complex and contradictory conditions of specific societies. As with all openings, it may be frightening to forsake the comfort of known terrain, whether theoretical or political. However, not to do so would be to forsake the opportunity for a reinvigorated Marxist analysis of the fundamentally important issues in the debate over the TRPF.

Notes and References

Chapter 1: Introduction

1. For a good selection of theorists advocating this approach to Marxian theory see Roemer (1986). Also see Elster (1985), Carling (1986) and Przeworski (1985).
2. This tradition would include such theorists as the early Lukács, Kautsky, Hilferding, Bernstein and Stalin among others. See Martin Jay (Introduction, 1984 and Alex Callinicos (Chapter 1, 1976) for good surveys of Hegelian Marxism.
3. Strictly speaking, accumulation is defined by Marx to be an increase in constant and variable capital, and may or may not embody a technical change. Marx defines accumulation of capital in volume I of *Capital* as 'The employment of surplus-value as capital, or its reconversion into capital, is called accumulation of capital' (1976, p. 725). In contrast, technical change involves a change in the manner in which a commodity is produced. In a two-factor world of capital and labor, a technical change would mean a change in the capital–labor ratio. The accumulation of capital might or might not also involve a technical change. A production process characterized by constant returns to scale (e.g. double all inputs and the output would also double) is one where the expansion of the scale of production involves the accumulation of capital but not a technical change. An accumulation of capital which leads to a rise in the organic composition of capital, however, is an example of accumulation that also is characterized by technical change. The difference between technical change and accumulation of capital are often confused in the literature. As is argued in Chapters 2 and 3, this confusion is due in part to the nonrecognition of the distinct paradigms at work in the debate over the TRPF.
4. For an extensive discussion of the tendency for the rate of profit to fall in Classical economics, see Tucker (1960).
5. This distinction between the *mass* of profit and the *rate* of profit was not always clearly made by Classical economists. Marx was one of the few who clearly argued that the rate of profit could fall while the

mass of profits rose. When referring here to the preMarxian, Classical theorists, the rate and mass of profit will be used interchangeably.

6. The fullest discussion by Marx of the tendency for the rate of profit to fall can be found in Chapters 13–15 of volume III of *Capital*.
7. Marx discusses the counteracting tendencies to a falling rate of profit in Chapter 14 of volume III of *Capital*.
8. See Howard (Chapter 3, 1980) for an insightful discussion of the neoclassical theory of income distribution.
9. See Jacoby (1975) for a useful discussion of Tugan-Baranovsky. See also Howard and King (1989, pp. 168–76).
10. See Jacoby for an extended discussion of Grossman's theory of crisis and the political implications of his theory. See Howard and King (1989, pp. 316–36) for a detailed analysis of the economics of Grossman's theory of capitalist accumulation and breakdown. Grossman's classic text has recently been translated from the German and published in English (1992).
11. In the 1970s a spirited and extensive debate on many of the traditional issues concerning the TRPF (including the interpretation of Marx's value theory, the nature of capitalist accumulation and the implication of a TRPF for a theory of crisis) occurred in the pages of the British journal *Bulletin of the Conference of Socialist Economics*, the precursor to *Capital and Class*. See, among others, the articles by Armstrong (1975), Catephores (1973), Cogoy (1973), Glyn (1972, 1973) and, especially, Himmelweit (1974). This debate in part acted as a bridge between the traditional debate over the TRPF and the debate over Okishio's theorem.
12. See the articles by Dobb (1959), Mattick (1959), Morris (1958), Pesenti (1959) and Robinson (1959).
13. See Shaikh (1978b, 1980) and Weeks (1982).
14. For instance, see Pat Clawson (1983).
15. Norton (1992) stresses that the inevitability of a falling rate of profit has important political implications for many who see the law of the TRPF as providing an objective basis for the transition to socialism. In a review of what he calls the 'productionist' approach to Marxian crisis theory he concludes that:

> The proposition that capitalism's fundamental nature expresses itself in unavoidable and growing crises (whether secularly, as for Yaffe, or in periodic long-wave downturns, as for Shaikh) is thought to be important not simply because it is scientifically correct; it is an insight which is politically essential, opening, as Grossman at least hoped, a third path between the embrace of capitalism, on the one side, and adherence to the twentieth

century's bureaucratically administered workers' movements, on the other. (1992, p. 162)

16. See Shaikh (1978b) and Weeks (1982).
17. Classical theories of epistemology have come under severe attack over the last thirty years across the disciplines. Post-structuralist and post-modernist theories have challenged the protocols and foundational bases of much of traditional philosophy of science and put forward 'social constructivist' theories of knowledge in place of the traditional correspondence theories of knowledge, namely rationalism and empiricism. Among many others, see especially Kuhn (1970), Rorty (1979), Foucault (1976), Goodman (1978), Derrida (1974), Toulmin (1990) and McCloskey (1985).
18. The rejection of classical epistemologies in many ways occurred in parallel fashion in the Marxian and nonMarxian traditions. In the last 30 years, Althusser (1975, 1979, 1982) has probably been the most influential in putting this anti-foundationalist position forward. His original work in the 1960s has led to a number of highly original and influential developments. See Amariglio (1987) for a detailed analysis of Althusser's rejection of 'science' as a master discourse. The early work of Hindess and Hirst developed a withering and sustained critique first of empiricism and then rationalism. In the end, they rejected the epistemological project altogether, as well as the approach of Althusser (see Hindess and Hirst, 1977a, 1977b, and with Cutler and Hussain, 1977). Laclau and Mouffe (1985) have extended Althusser's concept of overdetermination and Gramsci's notion of hegemony to develop a 'post-Marxist' politics based on what they call 'radical democracy.' In economics, Resnick and Wolff (1982, 1987) have reconceived the Marxian theory of class in a nonessentialist fashion based on Althusser's concept of overdetermination.
19. See Althusser (1979) and Resnick and Wolff (1987).
20. See Althusser (1982, Part Three).
21. See Levins and Lewontin (1985, Conclusion).

Chapter 2: The Hegelian Totality and the Traditional Debate over the Tendency for the Rate of Profit to Fall

1. The concept of Hegelian totality which is developed in this chapter is based on a particular reading of Hegel and his influence on the Marxist tradition. There can be no doubt that there are numerous alternative readings of Hegel which do not emphasize the importance of totality and the theory of history as developed in the present

work. For influential and alternative readings of Hegel see, among others, Charles Taylor (1979), Alexandre Kojeve (1969), J. N. Findlay (1958) and W.T. Stace (1955). For alternative developments of Hegel's influence on Marx's *Capital*, see Tony Smith (1990) and Pichit Likitkijsomboon (1992). An alternative and influential 'Hegelian' reconceptualization of economic theory is David Levine (1977, 1978, 1981). See Norton (1986) for an elaboration and extended critique of Levine. For a recent collection of essays roughly in this tradition see Moseley (1993).

2. A good review of the origins of rationalist epistemology can be found in Cottingham (1988). See Robert Paul Wolff (1984, Chapter 2) for a good explanation of rationalism on Adam Smith's economics.

3. There have been a number of articles in recent years which have reported on empirical results concerning the TRPF. A non-exhaustive list of such studies would include Moseley (1988, 1990), Shaikh (1987), Dumenil, Glick, and Rangel (1987), Weisskopf (1979) and Edward Wolff (1979, 1986). There have been numerous other studies of the trend of the profit rate, which attempt to link the decline in the profit rate to all manner of causes. The empirical works referred to here are those which explicitly link a fall in the rate of profit to a rise in the organic composition of capital.

4. Indeed, following the Duhem-Quine thesis and recent work in the philosophy of science, the proof or refutation of a theory by empirical test has been increasingly problematized. See Blaug (1992) on Duhem-Quine and Pheby (1988) on the philosophy of science. McCloskey (1985) has been particularly influential in questioning the modernist proclivities of economics. Amariglio (1987) has likewise questioned the authority of science in Marxian theory.

5. The tradition of holism is discussed in detail in O'Neill (1973) and Phillips (1976).

6. Keynesian macroeconomics has been the subject of major debate in the last 20 years. The Keynesian orthodoxy of Samuelson, Patinkin and Solow (the so-called neoclassical synthesis) has been challenged by the new Classical school of Lucas, Sargent, Prescott and others for not providing adequate microfoundations to macroeconomic phenomena. Post-Keynesians have stressed the concept of 'fundamental uncertainty' and the aggregate nature of Keynes' economics. There have also been a number of economists who have investigated the epistemological and methodological foundations of Keynes (see especially Brown-Collier and Bausor, 1988, and Dow, 1985). For a good overview of the issues at stake in new Classical economics see Klamer (1984). For post-Keynesian economics see Eichner (1978).

7. See Schumpeter (1954, pp. 800–24) for an authoritative overview of the German historical school.
8. It should be emphasized again that this is only *one* reading of Hegel and, as will be developed shortly, *one* reading of Marx. The interpretation of Marx which will be presented seeks to capture his influence on Marxian economics in general, and the traditional debate over the TRPF in particular. Thus, I will not pay close attention to many nuances and complicated dialectical arguments of Marx's own writings. It is the Marxian tradition with which I am concerned here. Marx's arguments are presented only insofar as it helps to elucidate that tradition. There are, of course, numerous readings of Marx and Marxian dialectics. On one extreme there is Elster, who understands Marxian dialectics to be nothing more than the unintended consequences of individual choice (1985), and on the other hand there is the more Hegelian approach represented by Rosdolsky (1977) among others. The approach most closely associated with the present work is that following Althusser and Balibar (1975) and Resnick and Wolff (1987), both works which emphasize Marx's break from Hegel and the theoretical humanism (methodological individualism) advocated by Elster.
9. For a good overview on Hegelian Marxism see Martin Jay (1984, Introduction) and Alex Callinicos (1976, Chapter 1).
10. Elster (1985) and Roemer (1986) also criticize the teleology and functionalism of Hegel and Hegelian Marxism. In contrast to Althusser, however, who rigorously critiques Hegel and his influence on the Marxian tradition, Elster and Roemer simply reject Hegel as not adopting the methodological stance of 'modern' social science, methodological individualism and positivism.
11. Cohen (1978, Chapter 1) provides an especially lucid account of Hegel's philosophy of history. Indeed, perhaps too lucid, as Cohen himself points out, and therefore one which abstracts from much of the subtlety of Hegel's own analysis. Cohen's purpose, like that in the present work, is to make Hegel readily 'understandable' in order to explore some issues in Marxian theory, rather than to do full justice to Hegel's complexity. Needless to say, the approach otherwise taken by Cohen towards Marx is not the one being developed here.
12. See note 9.
13. Cohen (1978) argues that for Marx the superstructure is not as all-inclusive as is commonly understood. While this may be true, the purpose of this exposition of Marx is not textual exegesis, but rather the purpose is to lay out the commonly accepted understanding of Marx.

14. See Howard and King (1989) *passim* for the influence of the Second International on Marxian economics.
15. It should be noted that the law of the TRPF has not always been explicitly associated with Marxian crisis theory. That the rate of profit tends to fall as capitalism develops and accumulates need not engender crises, in part because such falls in the rate of profit will call forth counteracting tendencies which will tend to raise the profit rate, and in part because crises are a more complex phenomenon which involve cultural and political elements as well. Shaikh, in contrast, insists that the TRPF will eventually cause a crisis of capitalism. He differentiates between what he calls 'possibility' theories of crisis, such as underconsumption and wage squeeze theories, and 'necessity' theories of crisis, of which the principal example is the TRPF. The difference between the two types of crises is that possibility theories can be ameliorated through state policies, while the necessity theories cannot, so that 'in the capitalist dominated world the problems of stagnation and world-wide unemployment worsen over time' (1983, p. 142).
16. Bruce Norton has insightfully spelt out the role which accumulation has played in much of twentieth-century Classical and Marxian theory. In a series of highly original and detailed articles, he has critiqued the work of Steindl, Mandel, Baran and Sweezy, and Levine for their economistic and essentialist development of the laws of motion of capitalism and, in particular, the process of accumulation. See Norton (1986, 1988, 1992). The critique which Norton levels and the alternative which he begins to develop is taken up in Chapter 4 below.
17. It may seem strange to reference Fine and Harris, Althusser, and Hindess and Hirst in the context of defining capitalism as a Hegelian totality. Certainly, all of these authors are critics of Hegel and can be considered 'structuralist' in their approach to understanding capitalism in the works cited in the text. For the purpose of the argument being made here, however, structuralism can be understood to fall broadly within the theoretical ambit of the Hegelian totality as outlined above. The important point to stress is that structuralism understands structures as preexisting the individual parts of the totality and that it is the structures which give the totality shape and not its parts. Insofar as Marxian structuralism combines a synchronic structural logic with a diachronic developmental logic, it is similar to the Hegelian totality (see Fine and Harris, 1979).
18. The debate over the choice of technique in the present context can be traced to Okishio's original article (1961). Roemer has also made seminal contributions to this debate (1977, 1978). Shaikh provided a link between the choice of technique and a 'Marxian' notion of

competition in his controversial and influential article on Dobb (1978b). See also Steedman's (1980) and Shaikh's (1980) debate over Shaikh's original article. The choice of technique approach will be discussed in more detail in Chapter 3.

19. See Norton (1992) for an especially lucid treatment of the importance of accumulation on the Marxian debate over the TRPF.
20. A teleological explanation is one which seeks to explain an action by reference to the goal, purpose or 'telos' aimed at by an individual, group or system. Teleological theory can be traced back to the Stoics and has reappeared through the history of natural and social science. Teleology should be contrasted with strict mechanistic or Cartesian forms of explanation which 'viewed the universe as a mechanism functioning according to natural laws' (Mayr, 1982, p. 48). Mayr distinguishes between four types of teleology (ibid., pp. 48–51).

    1. Teleonomic activities are those natural processes which owe their behavior to a program. Physiological processes of individual development (ontogeny) and genetic programs are teleonomic as they are guided by a structure towards some endpoint.
    2. Teleomatic processes usually relate to inanimate objects in which a definite end is reached as a consequence of natural laws. A rock rolling down a hill does so not because of any intentional behavior but because of the laws of gravitation.
    3. Adaptive systems are related to functional arguments. The heart is built to pump blood through the body. Racism exists to divide the working class.
    4. Cosmic teleology applies the concept of teleology to the system as a whole, whether it be nature or society.

    Nature is assumed to have a purpose, it was created by design. Society and its history can be understood as developing according to plan in a teleological fashion. This is the form of teleology which has influenced Hegel and those Marxists who followed and adapted his logical system.

    It should be pointed out that teleological explanations can occur on the individual level as well (see Boudon and Bourricaud, 1989, p. 405). Intentional or purposeful behavior is often used as a justification or cause. Thus, the reason for a person entering a grocery store is to buy a loaf of bread. The intention of buying bread is understood as the cause for entering the store, not the fact that the individual put one leg in front of the other, for instance. Much of modern social science is based on teleological explanations of this sort which is commonly referred to as methodological individualism. The conse-

quences of this type of individual teleology for the debate over the TRPF will be taken up in Chapter 3.
21. Theories of cycles, stages or the breakdown of capitalism as teleological, in the sense that each phase or stage in the development of capitalism naturally leads to a new phase or stage where the previous stage is rejuvenated and the process begins anew. Hindess argues that 'a teleology combines an essentialism with a principle of temporal order (Hindess, 1977, p. 177). In their discussion of cycles, Boudon and Bourricaud point out the teleological element in various cycle theories (1989, pp. 100–3).
22. The cheapening of constant capital and the rise in the rate of surplus value will be discussed in detail below.
23. See Norton (1988, 1992) for an especially detailed and trenchant analysis of 'stage' theorists like Sweezy, Steindl and others. Also, see Shaikh's entry under 'economic crises' in Bottomore (1983).
24. See Hansen (1985) for a detailed analysis of Marxian theories of the breakdown of capitalism. See also Howard and King (1989, pp. 316–36) and Sweezy (1970, Chapter 10). Georgescu-Roegen in *Econometrica* (1960) provided a number of mathematical 'proofs' of the breakdown of capitalism.
25. In a multicommodity economy, capital would not be a homogeneous magnitude which could be represented as a scalar quantity, as there would be many types of heterogeneous capital. Rather, physical capital would be a vector of different capital goods. The same situation would apply to wage goods which are often used in definitions of the technical composition of capital to represent hours of labor worked. Thus, the technical composition of capital would be defined as a ratio of two vectors which is nonsensical. In order to compare the magnitude of capital goods to wage goods one must 'value' the heterogeneous bundle of capital and wage goods by some numeraire so that one can aggregate these various goods as a scalar value. Marx's value categories can be interpreted as doing just that. Morishima has interpreted Marx's value categories as just such aggregation multipliers (1973, pp. 87–104). The issue of the aggregation of capital led in the 1950s and 1960s to the famous 'capital theory' debate between the two Cambridges, Cambridge, England and Cambridge, Massachusetts. For an excellent account and analysis of this debate see Harcourt (1972).

In the present example, the issue of aggregation does not arise within the capital good and wage good sectors, as it is assumed that the capital good is homogeneous and so is the wage good. However, in order to compare the magnitude of the capital good to the wage good, each must be 'weighted' by the amount of socially necessary labor time needed to reproduce the commodity in question.

26. Each sector of the economy has a technical composition of capital, one for the capital good sector and one for the wage good sector. Thus, each sector has a measure of the technical composition of capital. By aggregating across sectors, the aggregate, or economy-wide, technical composition of capital can be calculated.

27. See Mandel (1978) for an extensive argument that constant capital and the organic composition of capital rose over the course of the twentieth century.

28. It is impossible to know the reason why the effect of productivity changes on wage goods were omitted from the discussion of the counteracting tendencies to the TRPF by virtually all commentators in the literature. Perhaps it is linked to the fact that Marx himself only remarked on the cheapening of the elements of constant capital in his discussion of the counteracting factors to the TRPF in Chapter 14 of volume III of *Capital* (1981, pp. 342–3).

29. See for example the article by Geert Reuten who develops a theory of the TRPF based on the 'stratification' of capital where old capital is devalued as new capital improvements are introduced:

> Therefore, because of the higher productivity of new plant capital relative to the previous stratification, its comparative profitability increases, along with a comparative profitability decrease (devaluation) of the rest of the stratification. Therefore, whilst the rate of profit of newly accumulated capital may increase relative to the capital just below it in stratification, even if its value composition is higher, the average rate of profit of the stratification decreases because of the average increase in the value composition of capital. (1991, pp. 90–1)

30. Fine and Harris certainly seem correct in their textual interpretation of Marx. While any text, especially *Capital*, can be read in different ways, it is difficult to reconcile the persistent overlooking in the literature of the distinction of Marx's concepts of the technical composition of capital, the organic composition of capital and the value composition of capital. Groll and Orzech (1987) also distinguish between Marx's three concepts of the composition of capital, although differently from Fine and Harris (1979). See the subsequent debate between Fine and Groll and Orzech over this issue (1990).

Marx makes clear the distinction between these three concepts in the first page of his famous chapter 'The General Law of Capitalist Accumulation' in volume I of *Capital*. As this distinction is so rarely recognized, it is worth quoting Marx in full. He writes there that:

> The composition of capital is to be understood in a twofold sense. As value, it is determined by the proportion in which it is divided into constant capital, or the value of the means of production, and variable capital, or the value of labour-power, the sum total of wages. As material, as it functions in the process of production, all capital is divided into means of production and living labour-power. This latter composition is determined by the relation of the mass of the means of production employed on the one hand, and the mass of labour necessary for their employment on the other. I call the former the value-composition and the latter the technical composition of capital. There is a close correlation between the two. *To express this, I call the value-composition of capital, in so far as it is determined by the technical composition and mirrors the changes in the latter, the organic composition of capital. Wherever I refer to the composition of capital, without further qualification, its organic composition of capital is always understood.* (1976, p. 762; emphasis added)

Thus Marx clearly makes a distinction between the value and organic compositions of capital. The organic composition of capital reflects Marx's recognition that the heterogeneous capital and wage goods need to be 'valued' in order to be aggregated. In order to capture the idea of increased mechanization involving an increase in the mass of capital goods relative to wage goods, Marx defines the organic composition in such a way that it 'mirrors the changes' in the technical composition. That is, Marx assumes unit labor values are constant in his definition of the organic composition of capital. The organic composition is in this sense a partial equilibrium phenomena. Marx, however, clearly recognizes that the increase in the technical composition of capital which occurs *pari passu* with mechanization will lead to a fall in unit values and thus he distinguishes the value composition of capital from the organic composition. In this sense, the value composition of capital refers to a general equilibrium adjustment.

It is to Fine and Harris' credit that they are among the very few to have recognized the importance of this difference in Marx and the implications that this then has for the discussion of the falling rate of profit in volume III of *Capital*. Certainly if Sweezy, Robinson, Meek, Rosdolsky, among others, had fully appreciated Marx's distinction between the organic composition and the value composition of capital, the issues of long debate over the cheapening of constant capital would have been clearer.

31. See Howard and King (1992), Chapters 13–15, for an excellent discussion of the development of Marxian value theory at this time.

32. Morishima first put forward what he called the 'fundamental Marxian theorem' which states that the rate of surplus value is positive if and only if the rate of profit is positive. The implication of this theorem is that there is no need to calculate surplus value in value categories in order to argue that there is exploitation in a capitalist economy. Knowing that the rate of profit is positive suffices to demonstrate that there is exploitation (1973, pp. 53–5).
33. See Weintraub (1979) for a good overview of this debate.

Chapter 3: The Debate over the Okishio theorem and the Cartesian Totality

1. The result of Okishio's theorem was not actually a new one. Something like Okishio's theorem can already be found in von Bortkiewicz (1952). Okishio himself credits his theorem to two obscure and neglected articles published in the 1930s by the Japanese economist Kei Shibata (1934, 1939). Indeed, the result of the Okishio theorem can be found in incipient form in Ricardo's *Principles of Political Economy and Taxation* (1976). In his chapter, 'On Machinery' Ricardo considered what the effect of a technical change on the distribution of income between the three great classes of capitalists, workers and landlords would be. Ricardo claimed the following.

    > The capitalist ... who made the discovery of the machine, or who first usefully applied it, would enjoy an additional advantage by making great profits for a time; but, in proportion as the machine came into general use, the price of the commodity would, from the effects of competition, sink to its cost of production, when the capitalist would get the same money profits as before, and he would only participate in the general advantage as a consumer, by being able, with the same money revenue, to command an additional quantity of comforts and enjoyments. (ibid., p. 263)

    Ricardo goes on to state that at first he thought all the classes in society would benefit materially from such an innovation; hence, the sinking prices of production and the same rate of profit as previously. However, as he later develops in the same chapter, there are a number of reasons why the standard of living for workers would not increase. Thus, assuming that the landlords do not manage to appropriate all of the extra surplus, the capitalists will enjoy higher profits. This analysis of Ricardo's is remarkably the same result demonstrated by Okishio 144 years later.

2. See van Parijs (1980) and Roemer (1977, 1979). Bowles (1981) provides a concise and insightful proof of Okishio's theorem. He recognizes, in contrast to almost all others who have accepted the validity of the Okishio theorem, that the theorem in and of itself does not disprove the TRPF. Bowles emphasizes that 'This result clearly does not disprove the tendency of the rate of profit to fall. It does, however, show that *under the assumptions used here*, no pattern of technical change (whether labor saving or not) can produce a lower competitive rate of profit as long as commodities exchange at their prices of production and the wage bundle is unaffected' (ibid., p. 186, my emphasis).

3. Groll and Orzech (1987, 1989a, 1989b) develop an invaluable genealogy of Marx's concept of the organic composition of capital and theory of the falling rate of profit. Furthermore, they claim that Marx had conceived himself of the general result of the Okishio theorem already in volume I of *Capital,* in Chapter 25, 'The General Law of Capitalist Accumulation'. In a footnote written by Engels to the third German edition, Engels notes the following which Marx wrote as a marginal note in his own copy of *Capital*:

> Note here for working out later: if the extension is only quantitative, then for a greater and a smaller capital in the same branch of business the profits are as the magnitude of capitals advanced. If the quantitative extension induces a qualitative change, then the rate of profit on the larger capital rises at the same time. (1976, p. 781)

Groll and Orzech take this as evidence that Marx anticipated the Okishio theorem. Certainly, Marx is referring here to the possibility of a rising rate of profit, but by itself that does not constitute sufficient evidence to claim that Marx anticipated Okishio's theorem. What Groll and Orzech miss is the fact that the Okishio theorem is part of a shift in ontological terrain, from the Hegelian to the Cartesian approach totality. To claim that Marx anticipated the Okishio theorem would require that Marx also would have accepted the Cartesian approach to totality, which is a dubious assumption at best.

4. See Descartes' *Discourse on Method* (1956) where he likens both the animate and inanimate world to a machine. Needless, to say this metaphor by Descartes in the seventeenth century has been one of the most profound and enduring metaphors in both the natural and social sciences.

5. For useful expositions of this school see, among others, Andras Brody (1974), John Broome (1983), Lynn Mainwaring (1984), Luigi Pasinetti (1977), John Roemer (1981) and Ian Steedman (1977).

6. M is the augmented-input matrix; that is, the matrix of the technical coefficients of production added to the matrix of the commodities comprising the real wage, bL. It can be seen that p is the left eigenvector of this equation and $1/(1 + r)$ is the eigenvalue. Assuming, as is commonly done, that M is a square, nonnegative, irreducible matrix, then a theorem of Perron–Frobenius guarantees that there exists an all-positive vector, p, which is associated with the maximum eigenvalue, $\alpha = 1/(1 + r)$. Thus, given the initial conditions, A, b, L, and competitive markets, there is an economically meaningful (i.e. no negative prices) equilibrium solution to this system of equations. See Pasinetti (1977, pp. 267–76) for a concise exposition of the applicability of Perron–Frobenius theorems to linear price of production models.
7. Some have argued that Marx's assumption of an equal rate of profit need not reflect a dynamic process of equalization. Rather, it is argued, Marx's modeling of the economy reflects a 'snapshot' of the economy at a particular point in time, and the equal rate of profit is just one such assumption of possible profit rate structures, and should not be understood as reflecting some underlying tendency towards equalization (see Wolff, Roberts and Callari, 1982). This claim, however, avoids the question of why this assumption is chosen to close the model and not some other one. It would appear that it is more than coincidence, thus reflecting some sense of the importance of the equalization of profits.
8. As will be argued below in detail, the linear price of production model and the Okishio theorem is part of the Cartesian approach to understanding the social totality. As such, a microfoundational approach should underlie any claim that is made about the movement of the profit rate, the nature of technical change and so on.
9. For proofs of the Okishio theorem see Okishio (1961), Roemer (1977) and Bowles (1981).
10. What some proponents of the Okishio theorem see as a strength in the requirement that capitalists base their decisions on technical change only on current prices, Shaikh sees as a fatal weakness. Shaikh argues that the nature of capitalist competition requires that capitalists must attempt to anticipate future prices in order to survive the competitive battle and minimize unit production costs. Failure to do so will result in extinction as other firms lower prices and drive those who have high production costs to bankruptcy (1978b, 234–5; 1980, 75). Shaikh's argument is explored in detail below.
11. See Norton (1992, pp. 159–62) for a similar position to the one taken here.

Notes and References 121

12. This argument concerning the eliminationist tendency of capitalist competition has strange bedfellows. A similar argument was made by Milton Friedman in his 1953 essay 'Methodology of Positive Economics' (pp. 19–23) and Armen Alchian (1950). It is a common argument made by Marxist economists as well. It is, however, a difficult argument to sustain, and one which requires a number of very restrictive assumptions. See Winter (1964) for a critique of the neoclassical argument. Cullenberg and Sinisi (1986) offer a critique of the Marxian argument because of its three-part reductionism of economy to firm, firm to capitalist and capitalist to simple gain-seeking behavior.
13. A Prisoner's Dilemma game is one in which individual rational players independently choose an outcome which is suboptimal, because each has an incentive to cheat, even though a preferred, or dominant, alternative is available through collaboration.
14. In this sense, game theory does not provide an alternative theoretical framework to the Cartesian approach underlying mainstream neoclassical theory. Game theory still requires preconstituted individuals who are social atoms sharing the same rationality. See Mirowski (1986, Chapter 7) for a critique of game theory where he argues persuasively that game theory does not provide a fundamental alternative to neoclassical theory nor an adequate basis for a new institutionalist economics.
15. See Mayr (1982, Chapters 2–3) for an insightful discussion of the development of biology and its interaction with the larger intellectual and social trends throughout its history. Mayr discusses biology's relationship to other natural sciences in these chapters as well.
16. See Wilson (1975) and Dawkins (1976) for influential and controversial works advocating the sociobiology approach.
17. See Lewontin, Rose and Kamin (1984), Levins and Lewontin (1985), Lewontin (1974), Levins (1968) and Stephen Jay Gould (1977) for extended criticisms of the sociobiology approach in particular, and the Cartesian approach to natural and social theory in general.
18. Levins and Lewontin's *The Dialectical Biologist* is a collection of essays written separately and jointly over a number of years. The book covers a wide range of topics including the theory of evolution, dialectics and reductionism in ecology, problems of Lysenkoism, agricultural research in the third world and the question of human nature. The underlying theme in these essays is a critique of the reductionism or Cartesianism at work in much of western theoretical and applied science. They counterpoise a dialectical approach to this reductionism which is explored brilliantly and clearly in the final chapter.
19. In an interesting parallel to Levins and Lewontin's metaphor of the clock in describing the Cartesian approach to understanding society,

Donald Katzner in a recent graduate level textbook in microeconomics uses the clock metaphor as a description of an economic model (1988, 6). Katzner's concern is primarily with the epistemological adequacy of rationalist deduction, while Levins and Lewontin are more concerned with the ontological primitives informing social and natural theory. Nevertheless, as Levins and Lewontin themselves intimate, there is a close relationship between these Cartesian ontological and epistemological metaphors.

20. See Cullenberg and Sinisi (1986) for an analysis of the role that the reduction of the individual capitalist to a single gain-seeking motive plays in linear price of production models and Marxian theory.

21. There are two distinct points which must be kept in mind regarding Hobbes. The first is that Hobbes helped to launch a Cartesian approach to social theory by understanding society from the perspective of a given human nature, namely the inherent drive of each individual to act in his/her own self-interest. The second point is that given this human nature there will result a societal war of all against all. This second point of the war of all against all is a necessary consequence for Hobbes of his individualism. For Hobbes, this less than socially optimal result of individualism could only be addressed by the state (see *Leviathan*, 1968). In contrast Adam Smith, who introduced the individualist approach to economics, argued that a well-defined set of property rights and competitive markets, what Smith called 'the system of natural liberty', would through the working of the 'invisible hand' transform Hobbes' societal struggle of all against all into a harmonious outcome (see *Wealth of Nations*, 1965). For an excellent analysis of the differences between Smith and Hobbes as applied to economics, see Sinisi (1992, 1994).

22. It is probably more correct to say that the approach of Edgeworth, which has subsequently been formalized by Debreu and Scarf (1963) as the theory of the core, better captures the idea of Smith and Hobbes of competition as a struggle which will lead to a social optimum. See Weintraub (1979, 1985) for an excellent history and appraisal of general equilibrium economics and the theory of the core. The general equilibrium approach following in the Walrasian tradition does not allow for an active role for the capitalist and therefore does not see competition as a dynamic process. See Cullenberg (1991) for a critique of such microfoundational models as applied to Marxian economics. The Austrian school of economic theory provides a similar, yet in many important ways different, critique of modern neoclassical Walrasian economics. See Kirzner (1973) for a good development of this position.

23. Hayek's arguments are collected and further developed in his book *Individualism and Economic Order* (1949). In a recent paper, Burczak (forthcoming) has argued that Hayek's individualism can be interpreted as falling within the realm of postmodern theory given the emphasis that Hayek placed on the inability of certitude and rational calculation. Burczak's argument should caution against a too simplistic coupling of individualism with Cartesian reductionism. However, there can be no question that methodological individualism and Cartesian ontological foundations often go hand in hand.
24. The debate over the Cartesian and holistic approaches to economics continues to occur in a number of applied fields in economics. For a careful analysis of one area of such debate, see David Ruccio's (1991) discussion of the contending structuralist and individualist schools of thought in development economics.
25. See the above section on the linear price of production model for a fuller description of the economy as Cartesian totality.
26. See Sinisi (1992, Chapter 1) for a meticulous description of the intellectual roots of what he calls 'individualism'. He traces individualism's roots to the Greeks and through the Protestant theology of Luther and Calvin. However, it is first only with Hobbes, and subsequently Adam Smith, that individualism began to take its modern shape as a political and theoretical doctrine. Hobbes' approach has been influential in modern microeconomic developments of Marxism. Bowles (1985) develops a Marxian model of the firm, which while distinctly different from the neoHobbesian approach, shares certain affinities with it, in particular its emphasis on conflict and struggle. The neoHobbesian approach essentializes the idea of struggle in human nature while, for Bowles, the Marxian approach understands struggle to be rooted in specific social relations, capitalist social relations in particular.
27. It should be noted that some make a distinction between microfoundations and methodological individualism. On the one hand, methodological individualism refers to the reductionist form of social explanation which states that all adequate explanation must take the self-constituted individual as a primitive. Methodological individualist theories then proceed from individual to totality in a deductive manner. Microfoundations, on the other hand, requires only a consistency between the micro and macro levels of theoretical explanation. For instance, it would be unacceptable to argue that on a macro level a firm's investment is determined by profitability, but insist that an adequate micro explanation of firm investment behavior has nothing to do with profitability.

Herbert Gintis argues in a similar fashion that traditional neoclassical economics is in fact not based on methodological individualism, despite the claim to the contrary by many neoclassical economists. He argues that:

> The actual methodology of neoclassical theory is to posit the existence of certain institutions (prices, markets, etc.) and attempt to show that they are compatible with the actions of individual agents ... This position may be understood as asserting that economic theory must have logically consistent microfoundations. (1992, p. 109)

He argues, correctly, that 'no one has shown that any particular social institutions are the logical implication of individual action', and that 'Economic theory is not alone in its inability to derive macrostructure from microstructure ... The quest for spontaneous emergence of structure has, by and large, eluded modern science, natural and behavioral alike' (ibid., p. 109). However, while neoclassical theory may not actually succeed in deriving aggregate results from individual agents (what is commonly referred to as the 'aggregation problem'), it does require that all adequate explanations begin from individual maximizing behavior, as opposed to alternative micropathways (Levine, Sober and Wright, 1987) or alternative social actors (Hindess, 1984). In this sense, neoclassical economic theory is certainly 'methodologically' individualist, if not in the reductionist sense as is commonly understood.

For Gintis, microfoundations should be embraced, but any claim to methodological individualism avoided. He applauds the analytical Marxists like Roemer, who have on the basis of a microfoundational approach 'disproved', among other things, Marx's theory of the falling rate of profit, as it contradicts the assumption of profit maximization. This may be. But Gintis overlooks the fact that critical to the Roemer/Okishio result is its assumption that the economy is structured as a Cartesian totality, and this way of conceiving of an economy is every bit as responsible for the rejection of the falling rate of profit as is the assumption of profit maximization. Indeed, as this chapter shows, there are those who posit an alternative microfoundations, as Shaikh does with his assumption of minimizing unit costs and cutthroat predatory pricing behavior, and who can still derive a falling rate of profit. Thus, it is both the assumption about the part (the capitalist) and the totality (economy) which determine the outcome of a theoretical proposition. Those who have recently made strong claims about the inadequacy of basic Marxian propositions based on the microfoundations approach must be clear that it is not just the assumption of profit maximization which produces certain results, but also assumptions about the structure and logic of the economy.

28. See Boudon and Bourricaud (1989, p. 405) on the teleology of intentional explanation.

29. See Sen's Presidential Address to the Econometric Society (1993) and his 'Rational Fools' (1977) article for a critique and defense of rational choice theory understood alternatively as consistent behavior or self-interested behavior.

30. Interestingly, Elster has been one of the leading theorists concerned with explaining the limitations of rationality and extending theories of causality to other non-rational motives such as weakness of will (akrasia), altruism, commitment and, more recently, social norms. See Elster (1983a, 1984, 1989d, 1989e).

31. Roemer reflects this position in a dismissive and hostile fashion when he writes that 'Too often, obscurantism protects itself behind a yoga of special terms and privileged logic. The yoga of Marxism is dialectics ... In Marxian social science, dialectics is often used to justify a lazy kind of teleological reasoning' (1986, p. 191). In characteristic fashion, Roemer does not offer any textual evidence for this dismissive claim (nor does Elster in his long book on Marx, *Making Sense of Marx*, 1985). Indeed, it is hard to imagine how anyone could accuse Lukács, Gramsci, Adorno, Althusser or Sartre, for instance, to be lazy thinkers, simply reciting incantations of the holy mantra of dialectics. Roemer and Elster's failure to confront seriously the texts of these and other authors leaves one to wonder who in the end are the lazy thinkers.

32. The self-evident appeal of methodological individualism which Elster defended with such exasperation in 1986 gave way soon to a more circumscribed position. In what surely must rank as one of the most striking changes of theoretical commitment, Elster has recently strongly qualified his once dogmatically held position on methodological individualism. As a result of studying collective wage bargaining in Sweden in 1985 (1989c), Elster came to realize, by his own admission (1989a, p. vii), that rational choice theory based on what might be called a 'pure' methodological individualism which sought to explain *all* social phenomena as in principle derived solely from individuals was not sustainable (1985, p. 5). Elster had discovered in the context of investigating Swedish collective wage bargaining that 'social norms' governing such things as concepts of justice and fairness were irreducible to individual rational choice. As he explained it:

> everything is up for grabs: the identity of actors, the rules of the game, the set of payoffs, the range of acceptable arguments. The

more I understood what was going on, the lower I had to set my sights. The initial aim of explanation [models based on rational choice theory] was gradually transformed into one of 'thick' phenomenological description. (1989a, p. vii)

Interestingly, Elster does not see a logical contradiction between methodological individualism and the existence of social norms which are irreducible to individual choice. In an article on 'Social Norms and Economic Theory' he wrote that 'To accept social norms as a motivational mechanism is not to violate methodological individualism ... Social norms, as I understand them here, are emotional and behavioral propensities of individuals' (1989b, p. 102). Thus, for Elster, it seems that social norms become just another argument in the utility function of a rational individual: 'To accept social norms as a motivational mechanism is not to deny the importance of rational choice' (1989b, p. 102). This is not the place to decide whether or not the presence of social norms vitiates the claims of methodological individualism as Elster claims Durkheim (1958) believed, but certainly the strong claim of the pure methodological individualist position referred to above is no longer tenable. Elster's relationship to methodological individualism has been aptly summarized by the sociologist Geoffrey Hawthorn. Hawthorn remarks that:

Having now, it seems, ended his tortured and enlightening tryst with rational choice, this is where Elster points. In this respect, he is at one with an increasing number of reformed methodological individualists, of philosophers and social scientists (and even a few of the broader economists) who hoped, only a decade or so ago, to derive a comprehensive explanation and a moral map from calculations of individual interest alone. (1990, p. 37–8)

This being the case, Hawthorn concludes, it may be time for Elster and others 'to take the idea of society seriously again' (ibid., p. 38). Or, as G.A. Cohen insisted a number of years previously in a debate with Elster on methodological individualism, 'Marxism is fundamentally concerned not with behavior, but with the forces and relations constraining and directing it' (1982, p. 489). Indeed, the long tortuous debate over the primacy of agency or structure, of methodological individualism and social norms, may be returning to Marx's original insight which he so brilliantly expressed at the beginning of the 'Eighteenth Brumaire of Louis Bonaparte'. Marx captured the tension between whole and part, Hegel and Descartes, structure and agency, methodological individualism and social norms in these famous words: 'Men make their own history, but not of their own free will; not under circumstances they themselves have chosen but under the given and inherited circumstances with which they are directly confronted' (1974, p. 146).

33. The claim that agency is incorporated in the approach of analytical Marxism in a meaningful way is a difficult one to sustain given the reductionist understanding of the individual which is put forward by Elster, Roemer and others. The general equilibrium approach of Roemer reduces the individual to a mere place holder in the system wide determination of the economy. The reduction of social aggregates to individual behavior, which Elster endorses, belies a structural causality wherein all social actors of the same type (i.e. capitalists or workers), behave in a like manner. For instance, to be a capitalist means to maximize profits and that behavior is given by the structural position of capitalist. See Cullenberg (1991) and Cullenberg and Sinisi (1986) for a critique of the notion of agency in the analytical, and other, Marxian models.

34. There can be no question that there has been more emphasis placed on the subject by Marxists in recent years. However, as the previous note argues, the subject is a relatively impoverished and centered one, no different in essence from the subject of mainstream economic theory. For a critique of this manner of bringing the subject back in, see Amariglio, Callari and Cullenberg (1989) and Cullenberg (forthcoming).

35. Elster emphasizes that 'Methodological individualism is about how social phenomena are to be explained, not about how they should be evaluated' (1985, p. 8). True enough, yet it would seem more than a coincidence that mainstream neoclassical economics is profoundly individualist in its method (utility maximization) and its overall social norm (Pareto optimality). Also, it is difficult to imagine that Hayek, one of the most ardent proponents of individualism as methodology and a libertarian in political philosophy, could have embraced anything but this couplet. It would be difficult, if not impossible, to conceive of Hayek, the methodological individualist, as also a partisan of the collective interests of the working class, against the capitalist class. Indeed, one would suspect Hayek would reject such a class distinction in favor of a contemporary update of Hobbes' war of all against all. In this case, Hayek's methodology certainly proscribes his political options, and rules out class-based politics as he would have to deny the very existence of classes.

36. In their recent book on Marxian methodology, *Reconstructing Marxism*, (1992) Wright, Levine and Sober agree with Elster and Roemer on the need to reject any trace of Hegelianism or holism from Marxian theory. They are 'sympathetic to the idea that what is distinctive in

Marxian theory is substantive, not methodological, and that the methodology adopted by Marxists ought to be just good scientific methodology' (ibid., p. 108). However, they reject the notion that methodological individualism is good scientific practice. Wright, Levine and Sober argue that one should seek micropathways to macrophenomenal explanations, but that the basic macro 'social types' cannot all be reduced to individuals. That is, they see other types of social actors which influence and determine macrosocietal results, and which cannot be reduced to individual behavior. Examples of such social actors would include firms, trade unions, governments, and so on. On this last point, Wright, Levine and Sober are close to Hindess (1984).

Chapter 4: A Decentered Marxist Approach to Totality and the Contradictory Movement of the Rate of Profit

1. Although the genesis of the idea of a decentered totality can be found in a number of authors (see Jay, 1984), the genealogy of the concept of a decentered totality can be usefully traced to Althusser (1979) and Althusser and Balibar (1975) and a number of others who built on their work. Barry Hindess and Paul Hirst develop in their jointly authored books with Athar Hussain and Anthony Cutler (Cutler, Hindess, Hirst and Hussain, 1977 and 1978) their critique of the notion of a structured or 'centered' totality and reject the concept of totality altogether in favor of what they call 'national economies'. Even though they drop the term totality, their approach has much in common with the approach of the decentered totality being discussed here.

   Resnick and Wolff (1987), Laclau and Mouffe (1985) and Laclau (1990) all critique the essentialist foundations the Hegelian and Cartesian totalities. In the essay 'The Impossibility of Society' in Laclau (1990) the traditional Marxist totality is deconstructed, and with it the notion of society as a structured and closed social object. He writes there that:

   > Each social formation has its own forms of determination and relative autonomy, which are always instituted through a complex process of overdetermination and therefore cannot be established *a priori*. With this insight, the base-superstructure distinction falls [and] the social only exists as the vain attempt to institute the impossible object: society. (ibid., pp. 91–2)

Diskin and Sandler (1993) raise important objections to Laclau and Mouffe's use of 'capitalism' and the 'economy' as unproblematic conceptual categories. They argue that Laclau and Mouffe are unable to completely break with essentialism because of this failure to interrogate the economy.

In an influential body of work, Fredric Jameson has also decentered the traditional Marxist notion of totality in his works *The Political Unconscious* (1981) and *Postmodernism or, The Cultural Logic of Late Capitalism* (1991). His work has opened up a growing interface between postmodernism and Marxism. This interface can be found, for instance, in many of the articles in the journal *Rethinking Marxism*, although the journal does not grow directly out of Jameson's work. For an insightful and sympathetic reading of Jameson, see Dowling (1984). Norton (1994) raises fundamental problems with Jameson's use of 'modernist' Marxist economic models that take their overall shape from the supposed inherent logic of capital accumulation. Norton, in this important critique, situates Jameson's economics in the Hegelian approach to totality and argues that Jameson's use of Mandel's concept of 'late capitalism' is inconsistent with Jameson's other theoretical concerns.

2. Althusser's essays 'Contradiction and Overdetermination' first appeared in French in the early 1960s. They were translated into English and published in 1969 in the volume *For Marx* (1979). Ever aware of the symptomatic nature of reading and the overdetermination of texts, Althusser writes in a special preface 'To My English Readers' that 'To understand these essays and to pass judgment on them, it is essential to realize that they were conceived, written and published by a Communist philosopher in a particular ideological and theoretical conjuncture' (ibid., p. 9). Given the highly controversial reactions these texts have engendered, it is worth bearing this word of caution by Althusser in mind. He goes on to state that these are *preliminary* texts whose goal is to investigate the concerns of the specific nature of the science and philosophy founded by Marx. This chapter can be understood as an attempt to extend the original insights of Althusser into the debate over the falling rate of profit in particular, and the nature of the economy in general. For good accounts of the development of Althusser's work as theoretical interventions see Amariglio (1987) and Andrew Levine (1981). For an excellent intellectual history see Elliot (1987).

3. See Resnick and Wolff (1982, 1987), Cutler, Hindess, Hirst and Hussain (1977) and Laclau and Mouffe (1985) for critiques of Althusser's use of concept of 'determination in the last instance'.

4. McIntyre (1992) traces the development of the concept of uneven development from its origin in the Soviet industrialization debates through its more contemporary usage in crisis theories and theories of imperialism. He argues that the concept has largely gone untheorized in the Marxian tradition despite its frequent usage. In the spirit of this chapter, McIntyre argues strongly for a nondeterminist understanding of uneven development.
5. Similar approaches to the decentered theory of the enterprise have been developed elsewhere. Most notable among these are Thompson (1982) and Cutler, Hindess, Hirst and Hussain (1978). While these approaches share much in common with the theory of the enterprise being developed here, they do not make use of the class analysis used in this chapter.
6. For further elaboration on this point, and a powerful critique of the use of accumulation as the essence of capitalist development, see Norton (1987, 1992).
7. Super profits are those profits which come to the innovating capitalist enterprise due to the increase in productivity. These super profits arise because the innovating enterprise can produce more use values in a given period of time and therefore realize surplus value from other capitalist enterprises. The realized rate of exploitation as used here refers to the ratio of surplus value and super profit earned by the enterprise relative to the enterprise's variable capital. As long as the unit values of the wage goods and capital goods in the economy are constant, the total amount of surplus value produced and the rate of exploitation will remain the same. This example assumes that the unit values are fixed and therefore the innovation leads to super profits.
8. Note that the unit values are assumed to stay the same here. Thus, the relevant concept of the composition of capital is the organic composition of capital and not the value composition of capital.
9. It is straightforward to show that $dSC/dSCs = -1$. Remember that $S = SC_a + SC_s$ where S is the fixed amount of already appropriated surplus value and therefore is a constant. This equation can be rewritten as $SC_a = S - SC_s$. By differentiating with respect to SCs, the result, $dSC_a/dSC_s = -1$, obtains.
10. It was assumed in Chapter 2 that there was a homogeneous wage good and a homogeneous capital good. This assumption is maintained here.
11. Technically, one should refer to the *value* composition of capital here, as this example assumes that the unit values of the wage and capital goods are variable. However, since the literature refers almost exclusively to the organic composition of capital, that name will be maintained.

12. This complex process of adjustment of unit values is similar to the metaphor used in the Okishio approach. The difference is that in the Okishio theorem, and in the linear price of production models on which it is based, this adjustment process is assumed to tend to an equal rate of profit equilibrium, while no such equilibrium result is being assumed here. See Cullenberg and Sinisi (1986) for a critique of the equilibrium adjustment process of linear price of production models.

13. The profits of an enterprise are always contingent, dependent on specific cultural (the ever changing discourse on accounting rules), political (the rules of a forever changing tax code) and economic (the flows of changing subsumed class distributions) processes. To see the importance of this note that profits can be defined as: Profit = S − SC_i. Profit takes on different meanings depending on what is and is not included in the term SC_i. For instance, the meaning of profit will vary greatly depending on whether dividend payments are understood as a 'cost' of doing business or as a part of surplus value. The decision to account for dividend payments, in one way or the other, depends of course on accounting rules, tax laws and the nature of corporate governance (i.e. who controls the firm, the managers or the stockholders). The rate of profit then is merely one index of the health of the capitalist enterprise. Another would be Profits/(C + V) and there need be no necessary correspondence between the two: for instance, the value rate of profit, S/(C + V), could rise, while the rate of profit, Profit/(C + V) falls (where Profit is defined differently than S) and the enterprise goes bankrupt.

Bibliography

Addis, Laird, 'The Individual and the Marxist Philosophy of History', in *Readings in the Philosophy of the Social Sciences*, ed. May Brodbeck, New York: Macmillan, 1968: 317–35.

Agassi, Joseph, 'Methodological Individualism', *The British Journal of Sociology* 11, no. 3 (September 1960): 244–70.

Alberro, Jose and Persky, Joseph, 'The Simple Analytics of Falling Profit Rates, Okishio's Theorem and Fixed Capital', *Review of Radical Political Economics* 11, no. 3 (Fall 1979): 37–41.

Alchian, Armen, 'Uncertainty, Evolution, and Economic Theory', *Journal of Political Economy* 58 (June 1950): 211–21.

Althusser, Louis, *Essays in Self-Criticism*, London: New Left Books, 1975.

—— *For Marx*, London: Verso, 1979.

—— *Politics and History*, London: Verso, 1982.

Althusser, Louis and Balibar, Etienne, *Reading 'Capital'*, London: Verso, 1979.

Amariglio, Jack, 'Marxism Against Economic Science: Althusser's Legacy', in *Research in Political Economy* 10 (1987): 159–94.

Amariglio, Jack, Callari, Antonio and Cullenberg, Stephen, 'Analytical Marxism: A Critical Overview', *Review of Social Economy* 47, no. 4 (Winter 1989): 415–32.

Applebaum, Richard, 'Marx's Theory of the Falling Rate of Profit: Towards a Dialectical Analysis of Structural Social Change', *American Sociological Review* 43, no.1 (February 1978): 67–86.

Aristotle, *Politics*, trans. B. Jowett, Oxford: Oxford University Press, 1920.

—— *Physics, the Works of Aristotle* (volume 2), ed. W.D. Ross, trans. R.P. Hardie and R.K. Gaye, Oxford: Oxford University Press, 1936.

Armstrong, Philip, 'Accumulation of Capital, the Rate of Profit, and Crisis', *Bulletin of the Conference of Socialist Economists* 11 (1975): 1–17.

Armstrong, Philip and Glyn, Andrew, 'The Falling Rate of Profit and Oligopoly: A Comment on Shaikh', *Cambridge Journal of Economics* 4 (1980): 69–70.

Arrow, Kenneth and Debreu, Gerard, 'Existence of Equilibrium for a Competitive Economy', *Econometrica* 22 (1954): 265–90.

Arrow, Kenneth and Hahn, F.H, *General Competitive Analysis*, San Francisco: Holden-Day, 1971.

Attewell, Paul, *Radical Political Economy Since the Sixties*, New Brunswick, NJ: Rutgers University Press, 1984.
Baran, Paul and Sweezy, Paul, *Monopoly Capital*, Harmondsworth, England: Penguin Books, 1975.
Bell, Peter, 'Marxist Theory, Class Struggle, and the Crisis of Capitalism', in *The Subtle Anatomy of Capitalism*, ed. Jesse Schwartz, Santa Monica, CA: Goodyear Publishing, 1977, 170–94.
Berger, Johannes and Offe, Claus, 'Functionalism versus Rational Choice', *Theory and Society* 11 (1982): 521–6.
Bidard, C., 'The Falling Rate of Profit and Joint Production', *Cambridge Journal of Economics* 12, no.4 (1988): 355–60.
Blaug, Mark, 'Technical Change and Marxian Economics', *Kyklos* 13, no. 4 (1960)· 495–512.
—— *The Methodology of Economics: Or How Economists Explain*, Cambridge: Cambridge University Press, 1992.
Bleaney, Michael, 'Maurice Dobb's Theory of Crisis: A Comment', *Cambridge Journal of Economics* 4 (1980): 71–3.
Bohm, David, *Wholeness and the Implicate Order*, London: Ark Paperbacks, 1983.
Bortkiewicz, Ladislaus von, 'Value and Price in the Marxian System', *International Economic Papers* 2 (1952): 5–60.
Bose, Arun, *Marxian and Post-Marxian Political Economy*, London: Penguin Books, 1975.
Bottomore, Tom, *A Dictionary of Marxist Thought*, Cambridge: Harvard University Press, 1983.
Boudin, Louis, *The Theoretical System of Karl Marx*, Chicago: Charles H. Kerr, 1915.
Boudon, Raymond and Bourricaud, Francois, *A Critical Dictionary of Sociology*, Chicago: University of Chicago Press, 1989.
Bowles, Samuel, 'Technical Change and the Profit Rate: A Simple Proof of the Okishio Theorem', *Cambridge Journal of Economics* 5 (1981): 183–6.
—— 'The Production Process in a Competitive Economy: Walrasian, Neo-Hobbesian, and Marxian Models', *American Economic Review* 75, no. 2 (1985): 16–36.
Brodbeck, May, 'Methodological Individualism: Definition and Reduction', *Philosophy of Science* 25, no. 1 (January 1958): 1–22.
Brodbeck, May, ed. *Readings in the Philosophy of the Social Sciences*, New York: Macmillan, 1968.
Brody, Andras, *Proportions, Prices and Planning*, Amsterdam: North Holland, 1974.
Broome, John, *Microeconomics and Capitalism*, London: Academic Press, 1983.

Brown-Collier, Elba and Bausor, Randall, 'The Epistemological Foundations of *The General Theory*', *Scottish Journal of Political Economy* 35 (August 1988): 227–41.

Bullock, Paul and Yaffe, David, 'Inflation, the Crisis and the Post-War Boom', *Revolutionary Communist* 3-4 (1975): 5–45.

Burczak, Theodore, 'The Postmodern Moments of F.A. Hayek's Economics', *Economics and Philosophy*, forthcoming.

Burman, Patrick, 'Variations on a Dialectical Theme', *Philosophy of Social Science* 9 (1979): 357–75.

Caldwell, Bruce, *Beyond Positivism*, London: George Allen & Unwin, 1982.

Callinicos, Alex, *Althusser's Marxism*, London: Pluto Press, 1976.

Carling, Alan, 'Rational Choice Marxism', *New Left Review* 160 (November/December 1986): 24–62.

Catephores, Georges, 'Some Remarks on the Falling Rate of Profit', *Bulletin of the Conference of Socialist Economics* 2, no. 2 (Spring 1973).

Cherry, et al., *The Imperiled Economy: Book I*, New York: Union for Radical Political Economics, 1987.

Christiansen, Jens, 'Marx and the Falling Rate of Profit', *American Economic Review* 66, no. 2 (May 1976): 20–6.

Chung, Joseph, *La Théorie de la Baisse Tendancielle du Taux de Profit*, Louvain-la Neuve: Institut des Sciences Economiques, 1981.

Clawson, Patrick, 'A Comment on Van Parijs' Obituary', *Review of Radical Political Economics* 15, no. 2 (Summer 1983): 107–10.

Cogoy, Mario, 'The Fall of the Rate of Profit and the Theory of Accumulation – a Reply to Paul Sweezy', *Bulletin of the Conference of Socialist Economics* 8 (1973): 52–67.

Cohen, G.A, *Karl Marx's Theory of History*, Princeton: Princeton University Press, 1978.

—— 'Reply to Elster on "Marxism, Functionalism, and Game Theory"', *Theory and Society* 11 (1982): 483–95.

Collier, Andrew, 'Aristotelian Marx', *Inquiry* 29 no. 4 (December 1986): 459–70.

Coram, B.T., 'Marx, Roemer and the Theory of the Falling Rate of Profit', *Australian Economic Papers* 25 (December 1986).

Cornforth, Maurice, *Historical Materialism*, New York: International Publishers, 1954.

Cottingham, John, *The Rationalists*, Oxford: Oxford University Press, 1988.

Cullenberg, Stephen. 'The Rhetoric of Marxian Microfoundations', *Review of Radical Political Economics* 22 nos 1 and 2 (1991): 187–94.

—— 'Exploiting the Individual: Allegories of Marxian Microfoundations', *Rethinking Marxism*, forthcoming.

Cullenberg, Stephen and Sinisi, John, 'The Microfoundations of Marxian Crisis Theory: A Critique and Reformulation', Discussion Paper # 25, Association for Economic and Social Analysis, University of Massachusetts, Amherst, 1986.

Cutler, Anthony, Hindess, Barry, Hirst, Paul and Hussain, Athar, *Marx's 'Capital' and Capitalism Today: Volume I*, London: Routledge & Kegan Paul, 1977.

—— *Marx's 'Capital' and Capitalism Today: Vol. II*, London: Routledge & Kegan Paul, 1978.

Davis, John, 'Keynes on Atomism and Organicism', *Economic Journal* 99 (December 1989): 1159–72.

Dawkins, Richard, *The Selfish Gene*, New York: Oxford University Press, 1976.

Debreu, Gerard, *Theory of Value*, New York: Wiley, 1959.

Debreu, G. and Scarf, H., 'A Limit Theorem on the Core of an Economy', *International Economic Review* 4 (1963): 235–46.

Derrida, Jacques, *Of Grammatology* Baltimore: Johns Hopkins University Press, 1974.

Desai, Meghnad, *Marxian Economics*, Totowa, NJ: Rowman & Littlefield, 1979.

Descartes, Rene, *Discourse on Method*, trans. Laurence J. Lafleur, Indianapolis: Bobbs-Merrill, 1956.

Dickinson, H.D., 'The Falling Rate of Profit in Marxian Economics', *Review of Economic Studies* 24, no. 2 (February 1957): 120–30.

Diskin, Jonathan and Sandler, Blair, 'Essentialism and the Economy in the Post-Marxist Imaginary: Reopening the Sutures', *Rethinking Marxism* 6, no. 3 (Fall 1993): 28–48.

Dobb, Maurice, *Political Economy and Capitalism*, New York: International Publishers, 1945.

—— 'The Falling Rate of Profit', *Science and Society* 23, no. 2 (Spring 1959): 97–103.

Dow, Sheila, *Macroeconomic Thought: A Methodological Approach*, New York: Basil Blackwell, 1985.

—— 'Beyond Dualism', *Cambridge Journal of Economics* 14 (1990): 143–57.

Dowling, William, *Jameson, Althusser, Marx*, Ithaca, NY: Cornell University Press, 1984.

Dumenil, Gerard, Glick, Mark and Rangel, Jose, 'The Tendency of the Rate of Profit to Fall in the United States, Part I', *Contemporary Marxism* 9 (1984): 148–64.

—— 'The Tendency for the Rate of Profit to Fall in the United States, Part II: The Pattern of Irreversability', *Contemporary Marxism* 11 (1985): 138–52.

—— 'The Rate of Profit in the United States', *Cambridge Journal of Economics* 11, no. 4 (1987): 331–59.

Durkheim, Emile, *The Rules of Sociological Method*, Glencoe, Ill.: The Free Press, 1958.

Eatwell, John, Milgate, Murray and Newman, Peter (eds), *Marxian Economics*, New York: W.W. Norton & Company, 1990.

Ehrlich, A. 'Notes on the Marxian Model of Capital Accumulation'. *American Economic Review* 57, no. 2 (May 1967): 599-615.

Eichner, Alfred (ed.). *A Guide to Post-Keynesian Economics*. White Plains, NY: M.E. Sharpe, 1978

Elliott, Gregory. *Althusser: The Detour of Theory*. London: Verso, 1987.

Elster, Jon, 'Marxism, Functionalism and Game Theory', *Theory and Society* 11 (1982): 453–82.

—— *Explaining Technical Change*, Cambridge: Cambridge University Press, 1983a.

—— 'Reply to Comments', *Theory and Society* 12 (1983b): 111–20.

—— *Ulysses and the Sirens*, Cambridge: Cambridge University Press, 1984.

—— *Making Sense of Marx*, Cambridge: Cambridge University Press, 1985.

—— 'Reply to Comments', *Inquiry* 29 (1986): 65–77.

—— *The Cement of Society*, Cambridge: Cambridge University Press, 1989a.

—— 'Social Norms and Economic Theory', *Journal of Economic Perspectives* 3, no. 4 (Fall 1989b): 99–117.

—— 'Wage Bargaining and Social Norms', *Acta Sociologica* 32, no. 2 (1989c): 113–36.

—— *Nuts and Bolts*, Cambridge: Cambridge University Press, 1989d.

—— *Solomonic Judgements*, Cambridge: Cambridge University Press, 1989e.

Ernst, John, 'Simultaneous Valuation Extirpated: A Contribution to the Critique of the Neo-Ricardian Concept of Value', *Review of Radical Political Economics* 14, no. 2 (Summer 1982): 85–94.

Feldstein, Martin and Summers, Laurence, 'Is the Rate of Profit Falling?', *Brookings Papers* 1 (1977): 211–27.

Findlay, J. N., *Hegel: A Re-examination*, London: George Allen & Unwin, 1958.

Fine, Ben, *Theories of the Capitalist Economy*, New York: Holmes & Meier, 1982.

—— 'On the Composition of Capital: A Comment on Groll and Orzech', *History of Political Economy* 22, no. 1 (1990): 151–5.

Fine, Ben and Harris, Laurence, *Rereading 'Capital'*, New York: Columbia University Press, 1979.

Foley, Duncan, *Understanding 'Capital': Marx's Economic Theory*, Cambridge: Cambridge University Press, 1986.

Foucault, Michel, *The Archaeology of Knowledge*, New York: Harper & Row, 1976.
Friedman, Milton, *Essays in Positive Economics*. Chicago: University of Chicago Press, 1953.
Gamble, Andrew, and Walton, Paul, *Capitalism in Crisis*. Atlantic Highlands, NJ: Humanities Press, 1977.
Gellner, Ernest, 'Explanations in History', *Proceedings of the Aristotelian Society* Supplementary volume 30 (1960): 157–76.
Georgescu-Roegen, Nicholas, 'Mathematical Proofs of the Breakdown of Capitalism', *Econometrica* 28, no. 2 (April 1960): 225–43.
Gibson, Bill and Esfahani, Hadi, 'Nonproduced Means of Production: Neo-Ricardians vs Fundamentalists', *Review of Radical Political Economics* 15, no. 2 (Summer 1983): 83–105.
Giddens, Anthony, 'Commentary on the Debate', *Theory and Society* 11 (1982): 527–39.
—— 'Marx's Correct Views on Everything', *Theory and Society* 14 (1985): 133–66.
Gillman, Joseph, *The Falling Rate of Profit*, New York: Cameron Associates, 1958.
Gintis, Herbert, 'The Analytical Foundations of Contemporary Political Economy: A Comment on Hunt', in *Radical Economics*, ed. Susan Feiner and Bruce Roberts, Boston: Kluwer Academic, 1992.
Glomblowski, J., 'A Marxian Model of Long Run Capitalist Development', *Zeitschrift fur Nationalokonomie/Journal of Economics* 43, no. 4, 1983.
Glyn, Andrew, 'Capitalist Crisis and Organic Composition', *Bulletin of the Conference on Socialist Economists* 4 (Winter 1972): 93–103.
—— 'Productivity, Organic Composition and the Falling Rate of Profit', *Bulletin of the Conference on Socialist Economists* 6 (1973): 103–7.
Goldstein, L.J., 'The Inadequacy of the Principle of Methodological Individualism', *The Journal of Philosophy* 53, no. 25 (December 1956): 801–13.
—— 'Two Theses of Methodological Individualism', *The British Journal for the Philosophy of Science* 9 (1958): 1–11.
Goodman, Nelson, *Ways of Worldmaking*, Indianapolis: Hackett Publishers, 1978.
Gould, Stephen Jay, *Ontogeny and Phylogeny*, Cambridge: Harvard University Press, 1977.
Gouverneur, Jacques, *Contemporary Capitalism and Marxist Economics*, Totowa, NJ: Barnes & Noble, 1983.
Groll, Shalom and Orzech, Ze'ev B., 'Technical Progress and Values in Marx's Theory of the Decline in the Rate of Profit: an Exegetical Approach', *History of Political Economy* 19, no. 4 (1987): 591–613.
—— 'Stages in the Development of a Marxian Concept: The Organic Composition of Capital', *History of Political Economy* 21, no. 2 (1989a): 57–76.

—— 'From Marx to the Okishio Theorem: A Genealogy', *History of Political Economy* 21, no. 1 (1989b): 253–72.

—— 'Capital–Labor Relations: Consistency of Complication? A Reply to Ben Fine', *History of Political Economy* 22, no. 1 (1990): 155–65.

Grossman, Henryck, *Das Akkumulations – und – Zusammenbruchs – gesetz de Kapitalistichen Systems*, Leipzig, 1929.

—— *The Law of Breakdown and the Capitalist System*, London: Pluto Press, 1992.

Hansen, F.R., *The Breakdown of Capitalism*, London: Routledge & Kegan Paul, 1985.

Harcourt, Geoffrey, *Some Cambridge Controversies in the Theory of Capital*, Cambridge: Cambridge University Press, 1972.

Harris, Donald, 'Accumulation of Capital and the Rate of Profit in Marxian Theory', *Cambridge Journal of Economics* 7 (1983): 311–30.

—— 'Are There Macroeconomic Laws? The "Law" of the Falling Rate of Profit Reconsidered', in *The Economic Law of Motion of Modern Society*, ed. H.-J. Wagener and J.W. Drukker, Cambridge: Cambridge University Press, 1986.

Harvey, David, *The Limits to Capital*, Chicago: University of Chicago Press, 1982.

Hawthorn, Geoffrey, 'The Fall of Economic Man', *The New Republic* (5 February 1990): 34–8.

Hayek, Friedrich von, 'Scientism and the Study of Society, Part I', *Economica* 9, no. 35 (1942): 267–91.

—— 'Scientism and the Study of Society, Part II', *Economica* 10, no. 37 (1943): 34–63.

—— 'Scientism and the Study of Society, Part III', *Economica* 11, no. 41 (1944): 27–39.

—— *Individualism and Economic Order*, Chicago: University of Chicago Press, 1949.

Hegel, G.W.F., *The Philosophy of History*, trans. J. Sibree, New York: Dover Publications, 1956.

—— *The Science of Logic*, trans. William Wallace, London: Oxford University Press, 1975.

—— *Phenomenology of Spirit*, trans. A.V. Miller, Oxford: Oxford University Press, 1979.

Himmelweit, Susan, 'The Continuing Saga of the Falling Rate of Profit – A Reply to Mario Cogoy', *Bulletin of the Conference of Socialist Economists* 9 (1974): 1–6.

Hindess, Barry, *Philosophy and Methodology in the Social Sciences*, Atlantic Highlands, NJ: Humanities Press, 1977.

—— 'Rational Choice Theory and the Analysis of Political Action', *Economy and Society* 13, no. 4 (November 1984): 255–77.

―――― *Sociological Theories of the Economy*, London: Macmillan, 1977.
Hindess, Barry, and Hirst, Paul, *Pre-Capitalist Modes of Production*, London: Routledge & Kegan Paul, 1977a.
―――― *Mode of Production and Social Formation*, London: Macmillan, 1977b.
Hobbes, Thomas, *Leviathan*, Baltimore: Penguin Books, 1968.
Hodgson, Geoff, 'The Theory of the Falling Rate of Profit', *New Left Review* 84 (March 1974): 55–82.
―――― 'The Rationalist Conception of Action', *Journal of Economic Issues* 19, no. 4 (December 1985): 825–51.
―――― 'Behind Methodological Individualism', *Cambridge Journal of Economics* 10 (1986): 211–24.
Hollander, Heinz, 'Das Gesetz des Tendenziellen falls der Profitrate, Marxen begrundung und ihre Implikationer', *Mehrwert* 6 (June 1974): 105–35.
Horowitz, David (ed.), *Marx and Modern Economics*, New York: Monthly Review Press, 1968.
Howard, Michael C., *Modern Theories of Income Distribution*, New York: St Martin's Press, 1980.
Howard, Michael and King, John, *The Political Economy of Marx*, London: Longman, 1985.
―――― *A History of Marxian Economics, volume I*, Princeton: Princeton University Press, 1989.
―――― *A History of Marxian Economics, volume II*, Princeton: Princeton University Press, 1992.
Hunt, Ian 'An Obituary or a New Life for the Tendency of the Rate of Profit to Fall?', *Review of Radical Political Economics* 15, no. 1 (Spring 1983): 131–48.
Hussain, Athar, 'Crises and Tendencies of Capitalism', *Economy and Society* 6 (November 1977): 436–60.
Itoh, Makato, *Value and Crisis: Essays on Marxian Economics in Japan*, New York: Monthly Review Press, 1980.
Jacoby, Russell, 'The Politics of Crisis Theory: Towards a Critique of Automatic Marxism II', *Telos* 23 (Spring 1975): 3–52.
James, Susan, *The Content of Social Explanation*, Cambridge: Cambridge University Press, 1984.
Jameson, Fredric, *The Political Unconscious*, Ithaca, NY: Cornell University Press, 1981.
―――― *Postmodernism or, The Cultural Logic of Late Capitalism*, Durham, NC: Duke University Press, 1991.
Jay, Martin, *Marxism and Totality*, Berkeley: University of California Press, 1984.
Kalmbach, Peter and Kurz, Heinz, 'Economic Dynamics and Innovation: Ricardo, Marx and Schumpeter on Technological Change and Unem-

ployment', in *The Economic Law of Modern Society*, ed. H.-J. Wagener and J.W. Drukker; Cambridge: Cambridge University Press, 1986.

Katzner, Donald, *Walrasian Microeconomics: An Introduction to the Economic Theory of Market Behavior*, Reading, MA: Addison-Wesley, 1988.

Kay, Geoffrey, 'The Falling Rate of Profit, Unemployment and Crisis', *Critique* 6 (1976): 55–75.

Keynes, John Maynard, *The General Theory of Employment, Interest, and Money*, New York: Harbinger, 1964.

Kincaid, Harold, 'Reduction, Explanation, and Individualism', *Philosophy of Science* 53 (1986): 492–513.

Kirzner, Israel, *Competition and Entrepreneurship*, Chicago: Chicago University Press, 1973.

Klamer, Arjo, 'Levels of Discourse in New Classical Economics', *History of Political Economy*, vol. 16, no. 2, 263–90.

Kojeve, Alexandre, *Introduction to the Reading of Hegel*, trans. James Nichols, Jr, New York: Basic Books, 1969.

Konus, A.A., 'On the Tendency for the Rate of Profit to Fall', in *Socialism, Capitalism and Economics Growth* ed. C.H. Feinstein, Cambridge: Cambridge University Press, 1967.

Koshimura, Shinzaburo, *Theory of Capital Reproduction and Accumulation*, ed. Jesse Schwartz, Ontario: DPG Publishing, 1975.

Krelle, Wilhem, 'Marx as Growth Theorist', *German Economic Review* 9, no. 2 (1971): 122–33.

Kuhn, Thomas, *The Structure of Scientific Revolutions*, Chicago: University of Chicago Press, 1970.

Kuhne, Karl, *Economics and Marxism: Volume Two*, New York: St Martin's Press, 1979.

Laclau, Ernesto, *New Reflections on the Revolution of Our Time*, London: Verso, 1990.

Laclau, Ernesto and Mouffe, Chantal, *Hegemony and Socialist Strategy: Towards a Radical Democratic Politics*, London: Verso Press, 1985.

Laibman, David, 'Technical Change, the Real Wage and the Rate of Exploitation: The Falling Rate of Profit Reconsidered', *Review of Radical Political Economics* 14, no. 2 (Summer 1982): 95–105.

Lash, Scott and Urry, John, 'The New Marxism of Collective Action: A Critical Analysis', *Sociology* 18, no. 1 (February 1984): 33–50.

Lebowitz, Michael, 'Marx's Falling Rate of Profit: A Dialectical View', *Canadian Journal of Economics* 9 (August 1976): 232–54.

—— 'The One-Sidedness of *Capital*', *Review of Radical Political Economics* 14, no. 4 (Winter 1982): 40–51.

Lerner, Daniel (ed.), *Cause and Effect*, New York: Free Press, 1965.

Levine, Andrew, 'Althusser's Marxism', *Economy and Society* 10, no. 3 (August 1981): 243–83.

Levine, Andrew and Sober, Elliot. 'What's Historical about Historical Materialism?', *Journal of Philosophy* (1985): 304–26.
Levine, Andrew, Sober, Elliot and Wright, Erik Olin, 'Marxism and Methodological Individualism', *New Left Review* 162 (March/April 1987): 67–84.
Levine, David, 'The Theory of Growth of the Capitalist Economy', *Economic Development and Cultural Change* 24, no. 1 (October 1975): 47–74.
—— *Economic Studies: Contributions to A Critique of Economic Theory*, London: Routledge & Kegan Paul, 1977.
—— *Economic Theory: The Elementary Relations of Economic Life*, Boston: Routledge & Kegan Paul, 1978.
—— *Economic Theory: The System of Economic Relations as a Whole*, Boston: Routledge & Kegan Paul, 1981.
Levins, Richard, *Evolution in Changing Environments*, Princeton: Princeton University Press, 1968.
Levins, Richard and Lewontin, Richard, *The Dialectical Biologist*, Cambridge: Harvard University Press, 1985.
Levy, David, 'The Impossibility of a Complete Methodological Individualism', *Economics and Philosophy* 1 (1985): 101–8.
Lewontin, Richard *The Genetic Basis of Evolutionary Change*, New York: Columbia University Press, 1974.
Lewontin, Richard, Rose, Steven and Kamin, Leon, *Not in Our Genes*, New York: Pantheon, 1984.
Likitkijsomboon, Pichit, 'The Hegelian Dialectic in Marx's *Capital*', *Cambridge Journal of Economics* 16 (1992): 405–19.
Lipietz, Alain, 'Derrière la Crise: La Tendance a la Baisse du Taux de Profit, L'apport QuelquesTravaux Français Récent', *Revue Economique* 33, no. 2 (1982): 197–233.
Lukács, Georg, *History and Class Consciousness*, Cambridge: MIT Press, 1971.
Lukes, Steven, *Individualism*, New York: Harper & Row, nd.
—— 'Methodological Individualism Reconsidered', *The British Journal of Sociology* 19, no. 2 (June 1968): 119–29.
Luxemburg, Rosa, *The Accumulation of Capital: A Contribution to the Economic Elucidation of Imperialism*, New York: Monthly Review Press, 1968.
Maark, Gerard, *An Introduction to Karl Marx's 'Das Kapital'*, New York: Oxford University Press, 1979.
Machlup, Fritz, 'Schumpeter's Economic Methodology', in *Schumpeter: Social Scientist*, ed. Seymour Harris, Cambridge: Harvard University Press, 1951.
MacIver, A.M., 'Levels of Explanation in History', in *Readings in the Philosophy of the Social Sciences*, ed. May Brodbeck, New York: Macmillan, 1968.

Mage, Shane, *The 'Law of the Falling Tendency of the Rate of Profit': Its Place in the Marxian Theoretical System and Relevance to the US Economy*, PhD Dissertation, Columbia University, 1963.

Mainwaring, Lynn, *Value and Distribution in Capitalist Economics*, Cambridge: Cambridge University Press, 1984.

Mandel, Ernest, *Marxist Economic Theory: Volume I*, New York: Monthly Review Press, 1970a.

—— *An Introduction to Marxist Economic Theory*, New York: Pathfinder Press, 1970b.

—— *Late Capitalism*, London: Verso, 1978.

—— 'Introduction', in *Capital: Volume III* by Karl Marx, New York: Vintage Books, 1981.

Mandelbaum, Maurice, 'Societal Facts', *British Journal of Sociology* 6 (1955): 305–17.

—— 'Societal Laws', *British Journal of Sociology* 8 (1957): 211–24.

—— 'Historicism', in *The Encyclopedia of Philosophy*, ed. Paul Edwards, New York: Macmillan, 1972.

Mandeville, Bernard, *The Fable of the Bees; or Private Vices, Publick Benefits*, New York: Capricon Books, 1962.

Marx, Karl, *A Contribution to the Critique of Political Economy*, New York: International Publishers, 1970.

—— *Theories of Surplus Value*, Volumes I-III, Moscow: Progress Publishers, 1971.

—— *Grundrisse*, New York: Vintage, 1973.

—— 'The Eighteenth Brumaire of Louis Bonaparte', in *Surveys from Exile*, ed. David Fernbach, New York: Vintage Books, 1974.

—— *Capital: Volume I*, Harmondsworth, England: Penguin Books, 1976.

—— *Capital: Volume III*, New York: Vintage, 1981.

Marx, Karl and Engels, Frederick, *The Communist Manifesto*, New York: International Publishers, 1982.

Mattick, Paul, 'Value Theory and Capital Accumulation', *Science and Society* 23, no. 1 (Winter 1959): 27–51.

Mayr, Ernst, 'Cause and Effect in Biology', in *Cause and Effect*, ed. Daniel Lerner, New York: Free Press, 1965.

—— *The Growth of Biological Thought*, Cambridge: Harvard University Press, 1982.

McCloskey, Donald, *The Rhetoric of Economics*, Madison: University of Wisconsin Press, 1985.

McKenzie, Lionel, 'On the Existence of General Equilibrium for a Competitive Market', *Econometrica* 27 (1959): 54–71.

McIntyre, Richard, 'Theories of Uneven Development and Social Change', *Rethinking Marxism* 5, no. 3 (Fall 1992): 75–105.

Meek, Ronald, 'The Falling Rate of Profit', *Science and Society* 24, no. 1 (Winter 1960): 36–52.
—— *Economics and Ideology and Other Essays*, London: Chapman & Hall, 1967.
Meikle, Scott, 'Marxism and the Necessity of Essentialism', *Critique* 16 (1983): 149–66.
—— *Essentialism in the Thought of Karl Marx*, La Salle, Ill: Open Court Publishing, 1985.
Mellor, D.H., 'The Reduction of Society', *Philosophy* 57 (1982): 51–74.
Miller, Richard, 'Methodological Individualism and Social Explanation', *Philosophy of Science* 45 (1978): 387–414.
Mirowski, Philip, 'Institutions as a Solution Concept in a Game Theory Context', in *The Reconstruction of Economic Theory*, ed. Philip Mirowski, Boston: Kluwer Nijoff Publishing, 1986.
Morishima, Michio, *Marx's Economics*, Cambridge: Cambridge University Press, 1973.
Morris, Jacob, 'Unemployment and Unproductive Employment', *Science and Society*, vol. 22, no. 3 (Summer 1958): 193–206.
Moseley, Fred, 'The Rate of Surplus Value, the Organic Composition of Capital, and the General Rate of Profit in the US Economy: A Critique and Update of Wolff's Estimates', *American Economic Review* 78 (March 1988): 298–303.
—— 'The Decline in the Rate of Profit in the Postwar US Economy: An Alternative Marxian Explanation', *Review of Radical Political Economy* 22, nos 2–3 (1990): 17–37.
—— *The Falling Rate of Profit in the Postwar United States Economy*, London: Macmillan, 1991.
—— (ed.), *Marx's Method in 'Capital': A Reexamination*, Atlantic Highlands, NJ: Humanities Press, 1993.
Mozkowska, Natalie, *Das Marxsche System*, Berlin, 1929.
—— *Zur Kritik Moderner Krisentheorien*, Prague, 1935.
—— *Zur Dynamik des Spatkapitalismus*, Zurich, 1943.
Nakatani, Takeshi, 'The Falling Rate of Profit and the Competitive Battle: Comment on Shaikh', *Cambridge Journal of Economics* 4 (1980): 65–8.
Nelson, Alan, 'Some Issues Surrounding the Reduction of Macroeconomics to Microeconomics', *Philosophy of Science* 51, no. 4 (December 1984): 573–94.
Nordhaus, William, 'The Falling Share of Profits', *Brookings Papers* 1 (1974): 169–217.
Norton, Bruce, 'Steindl, Levine and the Inner Logic of Accumulation: A Marxian Critique', *Social Concept* 3, no. 2 (1986): 43–66.
—— 'Epochs and Essences: A Review of Marxist Long-Wave and Stagnation Theories', *Cambridge Journal of Economics* 12 (1988): 203–24.

—— 'Radical Theories of Accumulation and Crisis: Developments and Directions', in *Radical Economics* ed. Susan Feiner and Bruce Roberts, Boston: Kluwer Academic, 1992.

—— 'Late Capitalism and Postmodernism: An Anti-Epochal Analysis', in *Post Cold War Marxism: Confronting the New World Order*, ed. Antonio Callari, Carole Biewener and Stephen Cullenberg, New York: Guilford Press, 1994.

Okishio, Nobuo, 'Technical Change and the Rate of Profit', *Kobe University Economic Review* 7 (1961): 85–99.

—— 'A Formal Proof of Marx's Two Theorems', *Kobe University Economic Review* 18 (1972): 1–6.

—— 'Notes on Technical Progress and Capitalist Society', *Cambridge Journal of Economics* 1 (March 1977): 93–100.

O'Neill, John (ed.) *Modes of Individualism and Collectivism*, London: Heinemann, 1973.

Parijs, Philippe van, 'The Falling Rate of Profit Theory of Crisis: A Rational Reconstruction by Way of Obituary', *Review of Radical Political Economics* 12, no. 1 (Spring 1980): 1–16.

—— 'Functionalist Marxism Rehabilitated', *Theory and Society* 11 (1982): 497–511.

—— 'Why Marxist Economics Needs Microfoundations: Postscript to an Obituary', *Review of Radical Political Economics* 15, no. 2 (Summer 1983): 111–124.

Pasinetti, Luigi, *Lectures on the Theory of Production*, New York: Columbia University Press, 1977.

Perelman, Michael, 'Marx, Malthus, and the Organic Composition of Capital', *History of Political Economy* 17, no. 3 (Fall 1985): 461–90.

Pesenti, Antonio, 'The Falling Rate of Profit', *Science and Society* 23, no. 3 (1959): 233–52.

Pheby, John, *Methodology and Economics: A Critical Introduction*. Armonk, NY: M.E. Sharpe, 1988.

Phillips, D.C., *Holistic Thought in Social Science*, Stanford: Stanford University Press, 1976.

Pippin, Robert, *Hegel's Idealism: The Satisfaction of Self-Consciousness*, Cambridge: Cambridge University Press, 1989.

Popper, Karl, 'The Poverty of Historicism, I', *Economica* 11, no. 42 (1944a): 86–103.

—— 'The Poverty of Historicism, II', *Economica* 11, no. 43 (1944b): 119–37.

—— 'The Poverty of Historicism, III', *Economica* 12, no. 46 (1945): 69–89.

—— *The Open Society and Its Enemies*, Princeton: Princeton University Press, 1950.

—— *The Poverty of Historicism*, Boston: Beacon Press, 1957.

Przeworski, Adam, 'The Ethical Materialism of John Roemer', *Politics and Society* 11, no. 3 (1982): 289–313.
—— 'Marxism and Rational Choice', *Politics and Society* 14, no. 4 (1985): 379–409.
—— *Capitalism and Social Democracy*, Cambridge: Cambridge University Press, 1986.
Reati, Angelo, 'The Rate of Profit and the Organic Composition of Capital in West German Industry from 1960 to 1981', *Review of Radical Political Economics* 18, nos 1–2 (1986): 56–86.
Resnick, Stephen and Wolff, Richard, 'Marxist Epistemology: The Critique of Economic Determinism', *Social Text* 6 (1982): 31–72.
—— (eds), *Rethinking Marxism*, New York: Autonomedia, 1985.
—— *Knowledge and Class*, Chicago: Chicago University Press, 1987.
Reuten, Geert, 'Accumulation of Capital and the Foundation of the Tendency of the Rate of Profit to Fall', *Cambridge Journal of Economics* 15 (1991): 79–93.
Ricardo, David, *The Principles of Political Economy and Taxation*, London: Dent, 1976.
Roberts, Bruce, 'Value Categories and Marxian Method: A Different View of Value Price Transformation', PhD dissertation, University of Massachusetts, Amherst, 1981.
Robinson, Joan, 'The Falling Rate of Profit: A Comment', *Science and Society* 23, no. 2 (1959): 104–6.
—— *An Essay on Marxian Economics*, London: Macmillan, 1963.
—— 'The Organic Composition of Capital', *Kyklos* 31, no. 1 (1978): 5–20.
Roemer, John (ed.), 'Technical Change and the Tendency of the Rate of Profit to Fall', *Journal of Economic Theory* 16 (1977): 403–24.
—— 'The Effect of Technological Change on the Real Wage and Marx's Falling Rate of Profit', *Australian Economic Papers* 17, no. 30 (June 1978): 152–66.
—— 'Continuing Controversy on the Falling Rate of Profit: Fixed Capital and Other Issues', *Cambridge Journal of Economics* 3 (December 1979): 379–98.
—— 'Innovation, Rates of Profit, and Uniqueness of von Neumann Prices', *Journal of Economic Theory* 22 (1980): 451–64.
—— *Analytical Foundations of Marxian Economic Theory*, Cambridge: Cambridge University Press, 1981.
—— *A General Theory of Exploitation and Class*, Cambridge: Harvard University Press, 1982a.
—— 'Methodological Individualism and Deductive Marxism', *Theory and Society* 11 (1982b): 513–20.
—— *Analytical Marxism*, Cambridge: Cambridge University Press, 1986.

Rorty, Richard, *Philosophy and the Mirror of Nature*, Princeton: Princeton University Press, 1979.

Rosdolsky, Roman, 'Zur Neuren Kritik des Marxschen Gestzes der Fallenden Profitrate', *Kyklos* (1956): 208-225.

—— *The Making of Marx's 'Capital'*, London: Pluto Press, 1977.

Rowthorn, Bob and Harris, Donald, 'The Organic Composition of Capital and Capitalist Development', in *Rethinking Marxism,* ed. Stephen Resnick and Richard Wolff, New York: Autonomedia, 1985.

Ruccio, David, 'When Failure Becomes Success: Class and the Debate Over Stabilization and Adjustment', *World Development* 19, no. 10 (1991): 1315–34.

Saad-Filho, Alfredo, 'A Note on Marx's Analysis of the Composition of Capital', *Capital and Class* 50 (1993): 127–46.

Salvadori, Neri, 'Falling Rate of Profit with a Constant Real Wage. An Example', *Cambridge Journal of Economics* 5 (1981): 59–66.

Samuelson, Paul, 'Some Notions on Causality and Teleology in Economics', in *Cause and Effect*, ed. Daniel Lerner, New York: Free Press, 1965.

Schefold, Bertram, 'Different Forms of Technical Progress', *Economic Journal* 86 (December 1976): 806–19.

—— 'Capital, Growth, and Definitions of Technical Progress', *Kyklos* 32, nos 1–2 (1979): 236–50.

Schroyer, Trent, 'Marx's Theory of Crisis', *Telos* 14 (Winter 1972): 106–24.

Schumpeter, Joseph, *History of Economic Analysis*, New York: Oxford University Press, 1954.

Schutz, Eric, 'Non-produced Inputs, Differential Profit Rates and the Okishio Theorem', *Review of Radical Political Economics* 19, no. 2 (1987): 43–60.

Schwartz, Jesse, *The Subtle Anatomy of Capitalism*. Santa Monica, CA: Goodyear Publishing, 1977.

Sen, Amartya, 'Rational Fools: A Critique of the Behavioral Foundations of Economic Theory', *Philosophy and Public Affairs* 6, no. 4 (Summer 1977): 317–44.

—— 'Internal Consistency of Choice', *Econometrica* 61, no. 3 (May 1993): 495–521.

Sensat, Julius, Jr, *Habermas and Marxism: An Appraisal*, Beverly Hills, CA: Sage Publications, 1979.

Shaikh, Anwar, 'An Introduction to the History of Crisis Theories', in *US Capitalism in Crisis*, New York: Union for Radical Political Economics, 1978a.

—— 'Political Economy and Capitalism: Notes on Dobb's Theory of Crisis', *Cambridge Journal of Economics* 2 (1978b): 233–51.

—— 'Marxian Competition Versus Perfect Competition: Further Comments on the So-Called Choice of Technique', *Cambridge Journal of Economics* 4 (1980): 75–83.

—— 'Economic Crisis', in *A Dictionary of Marxist Thought*, ed. Tom Bottomore, Cambridge: Harvard University Press, 1983: 138–42.

—— 'The Falling Rate of Profit and the Economic Crisis in the US', in Cherry, et al. (eds), *The Imperiled Economy: Macroeconomics from a Left Perspective*, New York: URPE, 1987: 115–26.

Shibata, Kei, 'On the Law of Decline in the Rate of Profit', *Kyoto University Economic Review* 9, no. 1 (1934): 61–75.

—— 'On the General Profit Rate', *Kyoto University Economic Review* 14, no. 1 (1939): 31–66.

Sinisi, John, 'Economic Struggles and Economic Development: Transformations in the Development of a Theme', PhD dissertation, University of Massachusetts, Amherst, 1992.

—— 'Marxism in the Shadow of Hobbes', in *Post-Cold-War Marxism: Confronting the New World Order,* ed. Antonio Callari, Stephen Cullenberg and Carole Biewener, New York: Guilford Press, 1994.

Smith, Adam, *An Inquiry into the Nature and Causes of the Wealth of Nations*, New York: Modern Library, 1965.

Smith, Tony, *The Logic of Marx's 'Capital': Replies to Hegelian Criticisms*, Albany: SUNY Press, 1990.

Sober, Elliot, 'Holism, Individualism and the Units of Selection', in *Proceedings of the Philosophy of Science Association Meetings*, ed. P. Asquith and R. E. Giere, Lansing, MI, 1981.

Sraffa, Piero, *Production of Commodities by Means of Commodities*, Cambridge: Cambridge University Press, 1960.

Stace, W.T., *The Philosophy of Hegel: A Systematic Exposition*, London: Dover Publications, 1955.

Stalin, Joseph, *Dialectical and Historical Materialism*, New York: International Publishers, 1940.

Stark, Werner, *The Fundamental Forms of Social Thought*, New York: Fordham University Press, 1963.

Steedman, Ian, 'Marx on the Falling Rate of Profit', *Australian Economic Papers* 10, no. 16 (June 1971): 61–6.

—— *Marx after Sraffa*, London: New Left Books, 1977.

—— 'A Note on the "Choice of Technique" under Capitalism', *Cambridge Journal of Economics* 4 (1980): 64–7.

Strachey, John, *The Nature of Capitalist Crisis*, New York: Convici-Friede, 1935.

Sweezy, Paul, *The Theory of Capitalist Development*, New York: Monthly Review Press, 1970.

—— 'Some Problems in the Theory of Capital Accumulation', *Monthly Review* (May 1974): 38–55.

—— *Four Lectures on Marxism*, New York: Monthly Review Press, 1981.

Taylor, Charles, *Hegel and Modern Society*, Cambridge: Cambridge University Press, 1979.

Thompson, Grahame, 'The Firm as a "Dispersed" Social Agency', *Economy and Society* 11, no. 3 (August 1982): 233–50.

Toulmin, Stephen, *Cosmopolis: The Hidden Age of Modernity*, Chicago: University of Chicago Press, 1990.

Tucker, G.S.L., *Progress and Profits in British Economic Thought 1650-1850*, Cambridge: Cambridge University Press, 1960.

Tugan-Baranovsky, M.V., *Studien zur Theorie und Geschichte der Handelskrisen in England*, Leipzig, 1901.

Wagener, H.-J. and Drukker J.W., *The Economic Law of Motion of Modern Society*, Cambridge: Cambridge University Press, 1986.

Walker, Angus, 'Karl Marx, the Declining Rate of Profit and British Political Economy', *Economica* 38 no. 152 (November 1971): 362–77.

Watkins, J.W.N., 'Ideal Types and Historical Explanation', *British Journal for the Philosophy of Science* 3 (1952): 22–43.

—— 'Methodological Individualism: A Reply', *Philosophy of Science* 22 (1955): 58–67.

—— 'Historical Explanation in the Social Sciences', *British Journal for the Philosophy of Science* 8 (1957): 104–17.

Watts, Martin, 'Microeconomic Theory: Should Radicals Steal the Neoclassicals' Clothes?', *Review of Radical Political Economics* 15, no. 4 (Winter 1983): 100–3.

Weeks, John, *Capital and Exploitation*, Princeton: Princeton University Press, 1981.

—— 'Equilibrium, Uneven Development and the Tendency of the Rate of Profit to Fall', *Capital and Class* 16 (Spring 1982): 62–77.

Weintraub, E. Roy, *Microfoundations: The Compatability of Microeconomics and Macroeconomics*, Cambridge: Cambridge University Press, 1979.

—— *General Equilibrium Analysis: Studies in Appraisal*, Cambridge: Cambridge University Press, 1985.

Weisskopf, Thomas, 'Marxian Crisis Theory and the Rate of Profit in the Postwar US Economy', *Cambridge Journal of Economics* 3 (1979): 341–78.

Weizsacker, Christian von, 'Organic Composition of Capital and Average Period of Production', *Revue d'Economique Politique* 87, no. 2 (1979): 198–231.

Wilson, E.O., *Sociobiology: The New Synthesis*, Cambridge: Harvard University Press, 1975.

Winter, Sidney, 'Economic "Natural Selection" and the Theory of the Firm', *Yale Economic Essays* 225 (1964).

Wolff, Edward, 'The Rate of Surplus Value, the Organic Composition, and the General Rate of Profit in the US Economy, 1946-1967', *American Economic Review* 69, no. 3, (June 1979): 329–41.

—— 'The Productivity Slowdown and the Fall in the US Rate of Profit, 1947-1976', *Review of Radical Political Economics* 18, nos 1–2 (1986): 87–109.

Wolff, Richard, 'Marxian Crisis Theory: Structure and Implications', *Review of Radical Political Economics* 10, no. 1 (Spring 1978): 47–57.

Wolff, Richard, Roberts, Bruce and Callari, Antonio, 'Marx's (not Ricardo's) "Transformation Problem": A Radical Reconceptualization', *History of Political Economy* 16, no. 3 (September 1982): 431–6.

Wolff, Robert Paul, *Understanding Marx: A Reconstruction and Critique of Capital*, Princeton: Princeton University Press, 1984.

—— 'The Resurrection of Karl Marx, Political Economist', *Social Research* 53, no. 3 (Autumn 1986): 475–512.

—— 'Methodological Individualism and Marx: Some Remarks on Jon Elster, Game Theory, and Other Things', *Canadian Journal of Philosophy* 20, no. 4 (December 1990): 469–86.

Wolfson, Murray, *A Reappraisal of Marxian Economics*, New York: Columbia University Press, 1966.

Woods, J.E., 'Okishio's Theorem and Fixed Capital', *Metroeconomica* 37, no. 2 (June 1985): 187–97.

Wright, Erik Olin, *Class, Crisis and the State*, London: Verso, 1979.

Wright, Erk Olin, Levine, Andrew and Sober, Elliott, *Reconstructing Marxism*, London: Verso, 1992.

Yaffe, David, 'The Marxian Theory of Crisis, Capital and the State', *Economy and Society* (May 1973): 186–232.

Zarembka, Paul, 'The Capitalist Mode of Production: Economic Structure', in *Research in Political Economy*, volume I, ed. Paul Zarembka, Greenwich, Connecticut: JAI Press, 1977.

Index

accumulation 5, 80; as inner law of motion of capitalism 14, 20, 31–4
accumulation effect 99
Adorno, T. 79
Agassi, Joseph 73
agricultural labor, declining productivity of 4
Alberro, Jose 61
Althusser, Louis 13, 14, 25–6, 31, 79, 80, 83, 84, 85, 86–90, 91–2, 95
analytical Marxism 76
Aristotle 21–2
Armstrong, Philip 66
Arrow, Kenneth 71, 73

Balibar, Etienne 26, 83
Baran, Paul 9, 36–7
Bausor, Randall 73
Bernstein, E. 30
Bleaney, Michael 66
Bohm, David 23
Bortkiewicz, Ladislaus von 6, 10
Bowles, Samuel 64
Brodbeck, May 73
Brown-Collier, Elba 73
Burman, Patrick 76
business cycle, theories of 34, 35

capitalism: theories of breakdown of 34, 37; theories of stages/epochs of 34, 36–7
capitalist competition 4, 10, 33–4, 62–4
capitalist enterprise *see* enterprise concept
capitalist fundamental and subsumed class processes 93

capitalist mode of production 31
Carling, Alan 76, 80
cheapening of constant and variable capital 40–4, 101, 103
'choice of technique' school 63, 64, 66
Chung, Joseph 20
classical economics 3–4
class process as entry-point 92, 96
Clawson, Pat 1, 53, 62, 64–5
Cogoy, Mario 35
Cohen, G.A. 31
comparative statics 57
competitive and optimality criteria 63–4, 66
contradiction 90–1, 97, 98
Cornforth, Maurice 30, 31

Debreu, Gerard 73
Democritus 68
Derrida, Jacques 12
Descartes, René 68
dialectic concept 25–7
Dickinson, H.D. 20, 32–3
disproportionality theory 6–7
Dobb, Maurice 20, 35, 62
Dow, Sheila 73
Durkheim, Emile 22

economic determinism 30, 88, 89–90, 92
economy concept 2, 16, 52–3, 86, 94, 95, 106
economy as machine 53–4, 56
Elliot, Gregory 91–2
Elster, Jon 50, 52, 55–6, 76, 77–81, 82, 83
Engels, Friedrich 11, 29–30

150

Index

enterprise concept 2, 16, 31, 32–3, 52, 70, 75, 85–6, 93–5, 104–5
entry-point concept 92
Epicurus 68
equilibrium configuration of economy 16, 57, 59, 64, 75
Esfahani, Hadi 61

Fine, Ben 31, 47–8, 53, 60, 65, 101–2
fixed capital 58, 60–1, 62–3
Foucault, Michel 12

game theory 64, 76, 82
Garegnani, Pierangelo 63
Gellner, Ernest 73
Gibson, Bill 61
Giddens, Anthony 82
Gillman, Joseph 9, 20, 49
Glyn, Andrew 66
Goldstein, L.J. 73
Goodman, Nelson 12
Gould, Stephen Jay 68–9
Grossman, Henryck 7, 11, 20

Hahn, F.H. 71
Harris, Laurence 31, 47–8, 101–2
Hayek, Friedrich 23, 72, 73, 76
Hegel, G.W.F. 21, 22, 23–8, 30, 78, 82, 84
Hindess, Barry 13, 31, 76, 79, 81, 83, 86, 89, 90
Hirst, Paul 13, 31, 79, 83, 86, 89, 90
historicism 22–3, 72
history, dialectical development of 26–7
Hobbes, Thomas 71, 76
Hodgson, Geoff 82
holism 19, 23, 72–3
Horkheimer 79
humanism, theoretical 80, 87
Hunt, Ian 53, 60

individualism 67–8
inner essence concept 15, 19–20, 25, 26

intentional explanation and methodological individualism 78–9
invisible hand metaphor 71

Jacoby, R. 7
Jay, Martin 22, 23

Kamin, Leon 68–9
Kautsky, K.J. 30
Keynes, John Maynard 22–3, 73
Kincaid, Harold 74, 76
Kuhn, Thomas 12

Laclau, Ernesto 13, 83, 86, 89
Laibman, David 61–2
Lash, Scott 76
Lebowitz, Michael 32, 47, 48
Legal Marxist school in Russia 6–7
Levine, Andrew 82
Levins, Richard 68–9, 75
Levy, David 76
Lewontin, Richard 68–9, 75
Lukács, Georg 24
Lukes, Steven 71, 73
Luxemburg, Rosa 7

McCloskey, Donald 12
Machlup, Fritz 71–2
McKenzie, Lionel 73
Mage, Shane 20
Malthusian population principle 4
Mandel, Ernest 20, 32, 37, 41, 42, 45, 46, 49
Mandelbaum, Maurice 73
Mandeville, Bernard 71
marginal productivity theory of income distribution 5
Marx, Karl 1, 3, 4–5, 6, 10, 24, 27–30, 31, 33–4, 39, 41–2, 44, 47–8, 73, 102
Mayr, Ernst 23
mechanistic causality 52, 57
mechanization 5, 7–8
Meek, Ronald 8–9, 10, 20, 39, 45–6, 49
Meikle, Scott 21–2

Mellor, D.H. 76
microfoundations approach 33, 55–6, 65, 66, 76, 77–8, 82
Miller, Richard 76
monopoly capitalism 9, 36–7
Morishima, Michio 49, 76
Moseley, Fred 20
Mouffe, Chantal 13, 83, 86, 89

Nakatani, Takeshi 61, 66
neoclassical economics 5, 10
Nordhaus, William 5

Okishio, Nobuo 6, 9–10, 46–7, 49, 51, 61, 62, 64
ontological individualism 75
organic composition of capital 5, 8–9, 30, 40, 47–8, 99, 102
overdetermination 86, 88, 90–1, 95–6

Parijs, Philippe van 10, 16, 53, 65–6, 76
Persky, Joseph 61
Plato 73
Plekhanov, G. 30
Popper, Karl 23, 72–3, 76
Prisoner's Dilemma games 64–5, 82
process concept 90–1
production of relative surplus value 44–8
profit maximization 10, 52, 55–6, 70, 75, 80–1
Przeworski, Adam 81–2

rate of exploitation 44–7, 99
rate of profit 95; defined 5, 10; movements in 105, 106
rational choice theory 52, 76, 78–9, 80, 82
rationalist epistemology 13, 19–21, 56, 89
rationality of capitalist, pregiven 52, 66, 75
redistribution of surplus value: in dynamic setting 101–3; in static setting 97–101

reductionism 52, 68–9, 73–4, 75, 78, 83, 104
reform versus revolution issue 7, 11–12, 106, 107
Resnick, Stephen 13, 79, 83, 86, 89, 90–2, 93, 95
Ricardo, David 3, 4–5
Robinson, Joan 7–8, 9, 10, 20, 41, 42, 44, 49, 101
Roemer, John 1, 49, 50, 55, 56–7, 61, 64, 66, 76, 77–8, 79, 80, 81, 82
Rorty, Richard 12, 13
Rosdolsky, Roman 8, 9, 10, 20, 37, 41–2, 45, 46, 49
Rose, Steven 68–9

Saad-Filho, Alfredo 101–2
Salvadori, Neri 61
Schmoller, Gustav 22
Schumpeter, Joseph 71–2
Second International 30
Shaikh, Anwar 10, 11, 53, 61, 62–4, 65, 66–7
sites concept 90, 91, 93
Smith, Adam 3–4, 33, 71
Sober, Elliot 82
Sraffa, Piero 49, 54, 76
Sraffian model 54, 64
Stalin, Joseph 30
Steedman, Ian 49, 63, 66, 76
structural determinism of individual agents 80–1, 82
structure in dominance concept 88–9
supervision effect 99, 102
Sweezy, Paul 7–8, 9, 10, 20, 32, 36–7, 40–1, 42, 44, 45, 46, 49, 101

technical change 2, 80
telos concept 19, 22, 25, 26, 30, 87
Toulmin, Stephen 12
Tugan-Baranovsky, M. 6–7

Urry, John 76

value composition of capital 47–8, 102
viable technical changes 58

Wagner, Adolph 22
Watkins, J.W.N. 73, 74
Weeks, John 10, 11, 37, 53, 59–60, 61, 62

Wolff, Richard 13, 79, 83, 86, 89, 90–2, 93, 95
Wolff, Robert Paul 82
Wright, Erik Olin 82

Yaffe, David 11, 33, 34, 37, 49, 59

Zarembka, Paul 33